INDIAN BEAD-WEAVING PATTERNS

The Author in buckskin, "Delaware" style. Narragansett Tribal Gathering, Charlestown, Rhode Island, August, 1982. Photograph by *Jack Szelka*.

INDIAN BEAD-WEAVING PATTERNS

•

Chain-Weaving Designs
Bead Loom Weaving
and Bead Embroidery
— An Illustrated "How-To" Guide

•

(Revised and Expanded Edition, 1989)

•

Horace Goodhue

•

BEAD-CRAFT | P.O. BOX 7435 | COTATI, CA 94931

Manufactured in the United States of America

Printing History:
Original Printing, 1971 – 3,000
Reprint of Original Title, 1974 – 5,000
Revised Edition, 1984 – 8,000
Revised and Expanded Edition, 1989 – 14,000
Reprint of Expanded Edition, 1993 – 20,000
Reprint of Expanded Edition, 2007 – 10,000

ISBN 0-961-35031-8

Library of Congress Catalog Card Number: 89-92095

Orders and inquiries should be addressed to the publisher at:

BEAD-CRAFT
Post Office Box 7435
Cotati, California 94931
U.S.A.

www.beadcraftbooks.com

Cover photo: *Mundy Studios*
Cover design and production consultation: *Jim Dochniak*

Cover bead-work is a "Flat Peyote Weave" design of the Eastern Cherokee. Chain-weaving by the author, *Horace R. Goodhue.*

CONTENTS

LIST OF ILLUSTRATIONS

Frontispiece:

The Author in buckskin, "Delaware" style. Narragansett Tribal Gathering. Charlestown, Rhode Island, Ausust, 1982. Photograph by *Jack Szelka.*

CREDITS

Obviously a collection of this sort could not be put together without the help and encouragement of a lot of people who should be mentioned. Unfortunately, in my case, there is no record of the names of most of the people I have met and been helped by over the years in which I have collected my bead patterns. In the text I have given personal credit wherever possible.

For this book I must acknowledge my debt to Indian friends who have given encouragement — including Maude Kegg (Ojibwa), Betsy Jacobs (Delaware), Rev. Marvin Red Elk (Lakota), Linda Snow (Seneca), and Ed McGaa (Ogalala) — who have encouraged me to continue this work. And, most especially, to my wife, Orpha, a skilled beader herself, who is very patient when beadwork sometimes takes precedence over other activities. Together we enjoy the company of friends who gather in our home to work on their beading.

My thanks go to my long time friend Cecile Malack, a skilled beader and an able assistant in my classes. I am glad that she — and a good number of others who have worked with me — have gone on to teach their beading skills to others.

I have had further encouragement from beaders, new beginners to long-time teachers, who have written to me about their use of my material and in some cases have given me valuable suggestions regarding corrections or additions to my work. My thanks to all of them.

Each tribe and geographical area has certain favorite patterns which are often unknown, or unused, in other parts of the country. I have learned these patterns by talking with Indians and doing bead-work beside them: Indians of North Carolina to Oregon, Arizona to northern Minnesota —Ojibwa, Lakota, Winnebago, Cherokee, Apache, Navajo and Crow are some. My thanks to them for trust and patience.

I have been using these patterns and designs in bead classes in my home, in the Minnesota Free-University program, and in classes sponsored by YMCA, YWCA, St. Paul Public Schools, University of Minnesota, Camp Fire and other groups. I have used them to teach young people to make their own items with the pride of good craftsmanship. I have been particularly pleased with the number of Indian youths who have appeared in my classes with an interest in the old craft which, for some reason, has not always come down to those who should inherit it.

PREFACE

My greatest satisfaction resulting from the earlier printings of this material has been in the personal responses of those who have written to me either to report success or to question some puzzling item. As this new printing reaches a still larger circle of bead-crafters I hope it will bring me more pleasant contacts.

I am often asked — "What do Indians think of you, a 'Wash-sheet-choo', doing and teaching their native craft." My answer: I have received friendship and respect from Indians in many parts of the country — a feather gift from a Tewa in Taos, a Hunkpapa pipe in South Dakota, welcome in private homes from northern Minnesota to New Mexico to North Carolina, invitations to dance at powwows as far afield as Seattle and Albuquerque, welcome at such affairs as the Crow Fair (Montana) and the Narragansett gathering (Rhode Island), and participation in the Ogalala Sweat Lodge ritual.

I feel that it is all based on my respect for their traditional craft and culture which started when, as a boy, I was in the now extinct "Lone Scout" organization and later, as a "Boy Scout", studying Indian crafts while working up to Eagle, Order/Arrow, Scoutmaster and Counselor.

As for myself, I regard bead-craft as both an interesting hobby and as a bridge of common interest over the generation gap between an elderly man and the dynamic youth of today who are developing a truer understanding of Native American history, culture and values.

August 6, 1989

Horace R. Goodhue

Horace "at work," Brownie group 1982

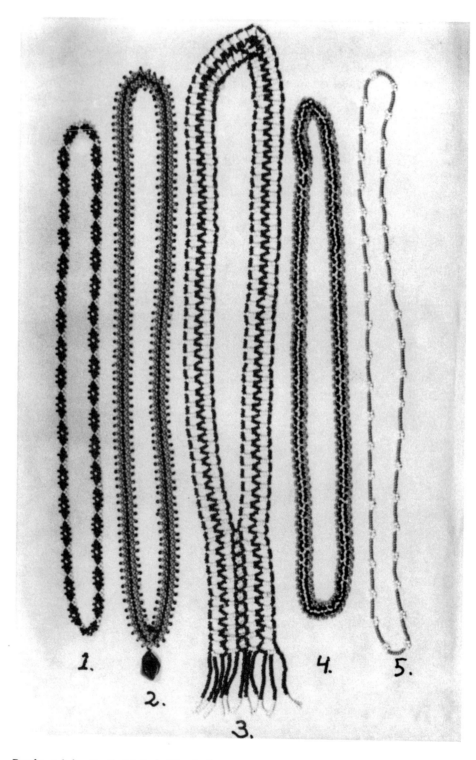

Bead-work by *Cecile Malack*. The designs are: 1. "Winnebago" 2. "Pointed Zig-zag" 3. 12-4-4" Zig-zag 4. "6-2-1" Zig-zag 5. "Daisies-on-a-string". Photograph by *Terry Schwab*.

"Look,

there's patience,

pride of accomplishment,

skill, knowledge, friendship

and happy occupation in this

bead-weaving, and there's no

one alive who can't benefit

from that list of

Positives."

(Dorothy Bix)

SUPPLIES

For teaching I usually use size #10/0 opaque seed-beads, and sometimes #7 or #5 pony-beads. Many Indians use the smaller size 11/0 and some even smaller than that. The best thread I have found is "Nymo" multi-filiament non-twisted nylon, size "D". To keep it from splitting or tangling I draw it several times across a ball of beeswax before using. There are various brands of good beading needles, 2 to 2 1/4 inches long. That is all you need to start beading.

You will gather equipment as you go along. Some mix bead colors together but keeping them separate is usually preferred. A little compartmented "picking box" is handy - such as hardware stores sell with small nails or for fishing flies. A nail clipper or razor blade in your picking box is handier than scissors. A dentist's probe is ideal for pulling knots and tangles apart. Then small pliers, tape measure and a supply of clasps, hooks or snaps.

In all free-hand weaving be sure to keep your work tight for good results. My instruction in class is - after adding a new unit, first pull up the old thread and then tighten the new thread.

Most of the patterns are good either as chokers or as longer necklace loops. Some also make nice bracelets or finger rings. As loops they can be worn with or without pendants. Good pendants are capped stones, small bells or ornaments of metal or ceramic. Small capped seashells are light and attractive. Lengths of beaded patterns can sewn to leather or cloth backing to make hatbands, headbands, chokers or bracelets. Nice-looking, practical, comfortable.

Use your imagination for new color effects and

ENJOY BEADING

Altho I have collected these patterns from many sources, the explanatory notes and diagrams (copyrighted) are strictly my own. Descriptive names I use are partly from Indians and partly "made up". I have grouped the patterns into main categories by similarity of technique.

So now let's start beading.

General instruction # 1 - always keep your thread pulled up tight to avoid sloppy work.

I. STRINGS

1. SINGLE STRAND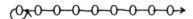

1a.   Simple - no instruction really needed yet. Many good effects can be obtained by mixing beads in size, shape and color. Also you can do some nice things with corn, squash, apple, watermelon or other seeds, or with small seashells.

1b.   Tasselled choker. Make main ring first, then add the tassels. Use faceted beads if available.

DETAIL

2. MULTIPLE STRANDS
2a.   Single strand to length desired, putting in an occasional larger bead.

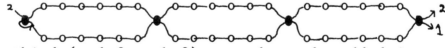

Add a second strand using the same larger beads.

A third (and fourth ?) strand may be added in the same way for a more elaborate effect.

2b.   OGALALA BUTTERFLY   I learned this pattern
from a young Lakota girl in Pine Ridge, South
Dakota.   Altho it is attractive and easily made,
it is not widely used.   It is a good one for
beginners as a bracelet or necklace.   Use double
thread in Step 1. for extra strength.

   Step 1.   Tie on one bead, then add more beads
to the desired length and tie in a large circle.

   Step 2.   Go on around the circle again, going
thru each 3rd bead. Add 3 new beads each time.

   Step 3.   Around the circle again, going thru
the middle beads of the previous "3's" while
adding 5 new beads each time.

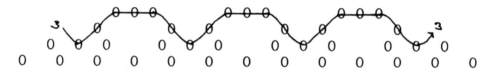

   Step 4.   Around the circle one more time, going
thru the middle beads of the "5's". For this Step
you add 7 new beads each time.

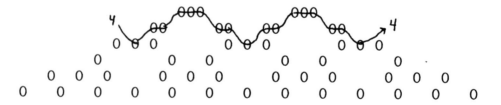

   Don't worry about the shape of it - it takes care
of itself.   I suggest using the same color for
Steps 2 and 3.   A beginner often finishes a
bracelet in the first session.

   See picture of the bracelet (#2,Page 31).

II. DAISY CHAINS

3.   DAISIES-ON-A-STRING   (Picture #5, Page 11)

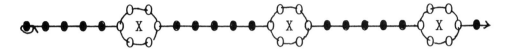

Start with a simple string of "●'s" (for the stem)
then add "○¹-○²-○³-○⁴-X⁵ " and BACK thru the first
"○ ". "X " will be the center –
you may want a different color.
    Pull it up to look like
Add "○⁶○⁷ " , back thru the last "○ ".
Pull tight and add the next stem group.

Repeat from the top for next daisy.
Sometimes the circle will seem
loose; if so, add a third bead
in the last step, ($O_6 O_7 O_8$).

4.   6-BEAD DAISY CHAIN
Sometimes called the "3-2" by Indian beaders –
it is the commonest pattern in most areas.

The most common variations are:

4a.	Dots
4b.	Circle-Bar
4c.	Diagonals
4d.	"Winnebago"

a. 0   0   0   0   0
   0   0   0   0   0   0
   ●   ●   ●   ●   ●
   0   0   0   0   0   0
     0   0   0   0   0

For the same results, some
Indians use the "4-1"
circular method and others
use either the "3-2" or
the "Potawatomi" weave
(explained later in #37).

b. 0   ●   0   ●   0
   0   0   0   0   0   0
      X   ●   X   ●   X
   0   0   0   0   0   0
      0   ●   0   ●   0

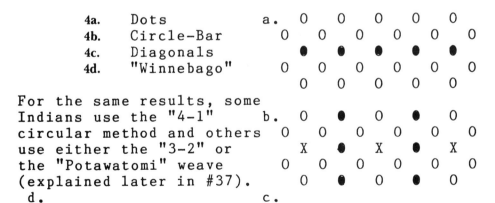

 I will explain the Circular "4-1" first.

CAUTION: I shall use the instruction "out thru the opposite bead". That is very important. It means that when you close a circle and then add a center by "crossing" the circle you must leave the circle thru the bead opposite to the one you entered thru. Going out thru the wrong bead will really mess it up. Please be careful.

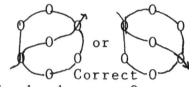

4a. DOTS: Tie a circle of 6 beads and add the center by going across

 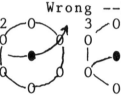 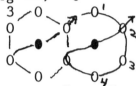

and out. You now have Fig.2 which is the "base" upon which the pattern will be built.

Step: Add "1 2 3 4", around and in thru the corner bead to form a new circle (Fig.3). Add "●" for new center, cross the circle and out thru the opposite. Keep on repeating this one Step. Now you have it right.   Right?

4b. CIRCLE-BAR: (Pictures: #8,P.23 & #5,P.31)
Base is same as shown for "4a" above   Step 1: Add"● 0 0 ●"

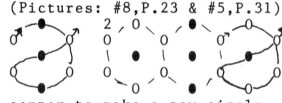

Go back in thru the corner to make a new circle. Add "●" for new center, cross the circle and go out the opposite bead.   You now have Figure 1.

Step 2: Add "0 0 0 0", in thru corner for new circle. Add new center "●", cross circle and out the opposite bead.   You now have Figure 2. Centers for base and Step 2 can be a third color

Continue by alternating Steps 1 and 2.

4c. DIAGONALS: (Pictures: #5,P.23 & #6,P.31)
Base: Make a circle of "● 0 0 ● 0 0", cross the circle adding "●" as center

Step 1: Add ● ● 0 ●, thru corner, add center 0, cross the circle and out thru the opposite bead.

Step 2: Add 0 0 ● 0, thru corner, add center ●, cross the circle and out thru the opposite bead.

These directions will give you alternate
diagonals in two colors. Using more colors is
very effective and not difficult. I will give
examples for 3-color and 6-color.

3-color diagonals (colors shown as 1, 2 and 3)
   Base: Pick up 2-3-3-2-1-1,tie circle,add center
2, cross circle and bring thread out thru 3.

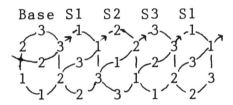

```
                          Base  S1   S2   S3   S1
Step: Pick-up:Center
   1.   1-1-3-2    3
   2.   2-2-1-3    1
   3.   3-3-2-1    2
Return to Step 1
```

6-color diagonals: Base same as in 3-color.
```
              Step: Pick-up:Center
                 1.   4-4-3-2    3
                 2.   5-5-4-3    4
                 3.   6-6-5-4    5
                 4.   1-1-6-5    6
                 5.   2-2-1-6    1
                 6.   3-3-2-1    2 ,back to St.1
```

   I am omitting diagrams here because I assume
that you are familiar by now with the basic
pattern thru doing the commoner variations before
trying the more involved ones.

4d. "WINNEBAGO" design made by "4-1" method.
(Yellow,Black,Red) Base: Circle of 6 R's,Cntr. Y.

```
         Step 1.   B-B-B-B , Center  R
              2.   Y-Y-Y-Y ,   "     B
              3.   Y-Y-Y-Y ,   "     B
              4.   Y-B-B-Y ,   "     B
              5.   B-R-R-B ,   "     R
              6.   R-R-R-R ,   "     Y
```

   Now let's study the "3-2" method of making
some of the "6-bead Daisy" designs. I have seen
this used in many places but I first learned it
from Rosalie Romero (Navajo) in New Mexico: she
said it is faster. You might want to experiment

with this as well as the "4-1" method (which you
already know) to see which one is easier, faster
and neater for you. Refer to the diagrams, page
15, to see what they are supposed to look like.

4a.   DOTS: Start with the same base that we had
before - the first circle and its center. Fig.a)

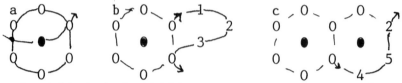

Step 1: Add 0 0 ● (123) & thru the corner (Fig.b)
Step 2: Add 0 0 (45) & go forward thru "2"(Fig.c)
        Continue by alternating the Steps.

4b.   CIRCLE-BAR: Same base as above in "4a". You
        can use a third color "X" for the center.
Step 1:   Add   ● 0 ● , go back thru the corner.
        (second bead back along the thread)
Step 2:   Add ● 0, go thru forward bead.
        (third bead back along the thread)
Step 3:   Add 0 0 X , back thru the 2nd.
Step 4:   Add 0 0 , back thru the 3rd.
        Repeat Steps - diagram on Page 5.

4c.   DIAGONALS: Base: ● 0 0 ● 0 0, tie in a
circle, add center ●.

Step 1: ● ● 0 , and
  back thru 2nd bead.
Step 2: ● 0, forward
  thru third bead.
Step 3: 0 0 ● , back thru 2nd.
Step 4: 0 ● , forward thru third. Repeat Steps.

For three colors; Base ● 0 0 ● X X , add center ●.

Step 1: X X 0 , back T 2nd
Step 2: ● 0 , frwd T 3rd
Step 3: ● ● X , back T 2nd
Step 4: 0 X , frwd T 3rd
Step 5: 0 0 ● , back T 2nd
Step 6: X ● , frwd T 3rd.   Repeat all Steps.

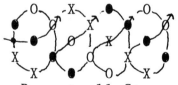

4d. **"WINNEBAGO"**

                        This distinctive design is often built by the "Potawatomi" weave which is explained later (on page 48 : directions for it on page 49). Actually the three weaving methods, "4-1", "3-2" and the Potawatomi are interchange- able and any design possible with one can also be made with either of the other two.

    Southwest Indians seem to favor "3-2", while in Wisconsin and Illinois the Potawatomi is well known.

4d. **"WINNEBAGO" BY "3-2" WEAVE:**

Traditional colors : "●"black,"R"red,"O"yellow

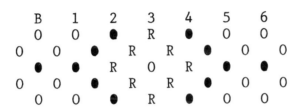

Base: circle of 000000, center ●
Step 1 0●● – 0●   Step 4 ●●R – ●●
Step 2 ●RR – ●R   Step 5 000● – 00
Step 3 RRO – RR   Step 6 000● – 00
Omit St.6 to bring figures closer together.

4e. **ALTERNATE CIRCLES:**
  Base: Circle of 6 0's with ● as center.

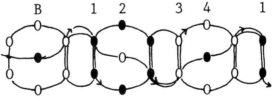

  Step 1: Add ● ●,
back thru 0 0, on
  thru ● ● again.

  Step 2: ● ● ● ●,
thru corner ●, add
center 0, and out thru the opposite corner bead.

  Step 3: 0 0, BT(back thru)
● ●, Thru 0 0 again.

  Step 4: Add 0 0 0 0, thru
corner 0, add center ●,   DETAIL OF
out thru opposite corner.   STEPS 1 & 3

4f.   EAR-DROPS

are very popular:
there is no limit to the nice
pieces you can make with
different types; small beads,
bugles and pieces of quill.
Notice that in this sample
the first open circle serves
as a loop for the ear-wire.

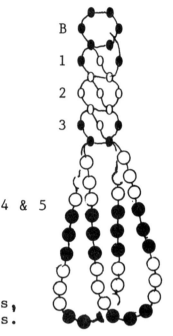

B
1
2
3

4 & 5

Base: circle of 6 $\bullet$'s, no cntr.
Step 1. $\bullet$00$\bullet$ + (center) 0
Step 2. 0000 + 0
Step 3. $\bullet\bullet\bullet\bullet$ + 0
Step 4. 30,3$\bullet$,30,3$\bullet$,30,3$\bullet$,30
Step 5. same as Step 4.

5.   8-BEAD DAISY CHAINS

Now, after the 6-bead daisies,
we meet another family of chains.

5a.   ALTERNATE CIRCLES: (#3,P.23)

Base: 8 $\bullet$'s in a circle, add
center X , across circle and out.
Step 1: Add 0 0, back thru old
$\bullet$ $\bullet$, again thru new 0 0. (same as
in "4e" DETAIL shown above)
Step 2: Add 6 0's , back thru
corner, add center X, out opposite.
Step 3: Add $\bullet$ $\bullet$, back thru old
0 0, forward thru new $\bullet$ $\bullet$ again.
Step 4: Add 6 $\bullet$'s , back thru
corner, add center X, out opposite.
Repeat from Step 1.

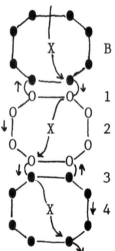

B
1
2
3
4

SUGGESTION: In an 8-bead circle,
the center bead is sometimes pretty
loose so some beaders use a double bead center
for firmer work; or put in a larger center bead.

CAUTION: I stress the word "opposite" because if
you come out the wrong bead when crossing a
circle the center bead will "hinge" out - see
top diagram on page 16.

5b. A popular and attractive "8-bead" alternate.

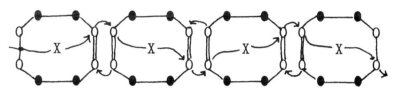

Base: Pick up 0 ● ● 0 0 ● ● 0, tie in a circle,
  add center x, cross the circle to opposite bead.
Step 1: Add 0 0, thru old 0 0, on thru new 0 0.
Step 2: Add ● ● 0 0 ● ●, thru corner, pick up
  center X, out thru the opposite bead. Repeat.

OTHER FORMS OF 8-BEAD CHAIN:

(first circle is base)

5c. Multiple repetitions of Step 1 gives this:

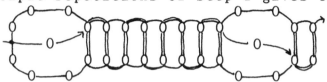

5d. With extra beads in Step 1 you get this:

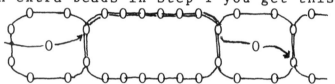

5e. Center line: Step 1,●●
     Step 2 00●●00, Cntr.●

```
 0 0     0 0     0 0
●   ●   ●   ●   ●   ●
    ●       ●       ●
●   ●   ●   ●   ●   ●
 0 0     0 0     0 0
```

5f. Arrows: Step 1 ●●
     Step 2 ●●00●●, Cntr.0
     Step 3 00
     Step 4 00●●00, Cntr.●

```
 0 0    ● ●     0 0
0   ● ●    0 0    ●
 ●       0       ●
0   ● ●    0 0    ●
 0 0    ● ●     0 0
```

5g. Multi-color: Three or
     more colors repeating.

Other ideas: Try larger
     center bead; or
     double centers.

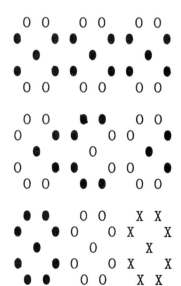

III. LADDERS

Two needles on the ends of a double length of thread are needed for ladder patterns.

The ladder technique: pick up the same number of beads on the two needles (these are the "side" units). Pass the needles in opposite directions thru the "rungs".   Keep your work tight !

6a. HORSE-SHOES: String 6 0's to the middle of a long thread with a needle on each end.

Step 1: Run both needles thru the same ● ● in opposite directions.
Step 2: Add ● ● to both sides.
Step 3: Run both needles thru the same 0 0 in opposite directions.
Step 4: Add 0 0 to both sides.
                Repeat from Step 1.

Alternate design –

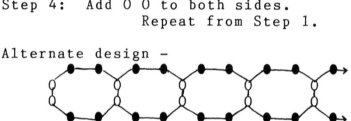

6b. LADDERS (as a class) Pick out a number for the "sides" and another for crossovers ("rungs"). Long thread, two needles and away you go. Some examples –

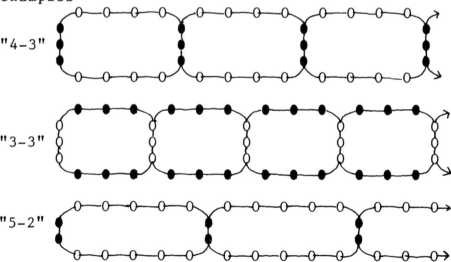

"4-3"

"3-3"

"5-2"

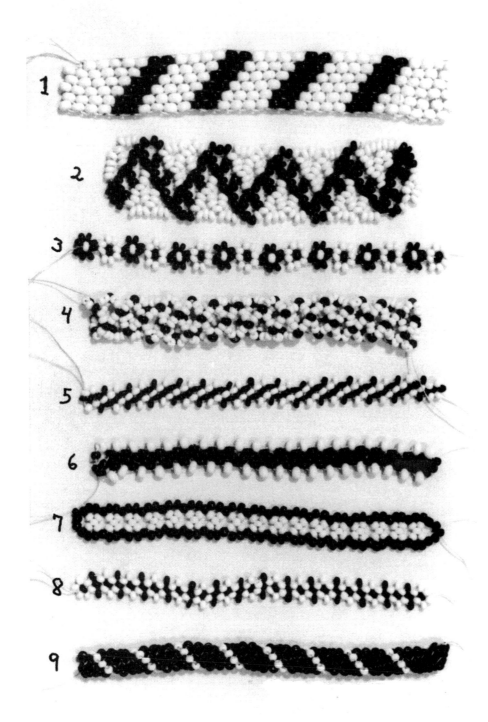

Bead-work by *Orpha Goodhue*. The designs are: 1. "Flat Peyote" 2. "Double Zig-zag" 3. "8-bead" Circles 4. "Lacy Tube" 5. "5-bead" Diagonals 6. "3-1-1" Zig-zag 7. "Bordered Crosses" 8. "6-bead" Daisy-Bar 9. Spiral "Peyote Tube" Photography by *Terry Schwab*.

FANCY LADDERS

7a.   RINGS: Several of the ladders make good
finger rings; for example, the "0-3".
When the correct length is reached go
back thru the first set of 3 and tie
securely.   It's easy to do.

7b.   LADDERS WITH BUGLES: Delicate ladders can
be made by combining bugles with regular beads.

Bugles with "oat" pearls

Bugles and luster pearls

Or try a "pointed" ladder with bugles

7c.   WOVEN LADDER: After completing a regular
ladder, weave separate single strings in and out
between the rungs.

7d.   THREE-SIDED:

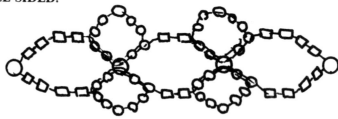

Three or more units long,   ROUTING OF THREAD
this makes an attractive
ear-drop.   Not really a
ladder since it is easier
to do one side at a time.

Use larger beads along the center line.   Make the
second side so it will look like the diagram.
Then go thru it again with a third side hooked
into the same center line.   I like white center
beads, light green for ◘ 's, red   0 's.

7e. OTHER LADDER VARIATIONS

Seed beads combined with "ponies"

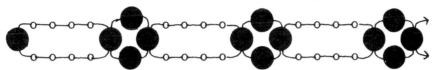

Four strings

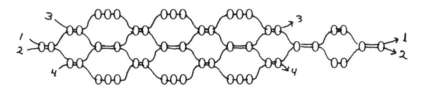

8a. BORDERED CROSSES:
This is an attractive elaboration of a basic ladder. I found it in Arizona. Start with a "3-1" ladder as the base.

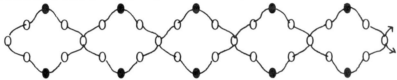

Instructions on Page 22. Build it to desired length (or to complete a large loop), then go along each side adding ● ● between each two edge ●'s. Note – this will make it a little shorter. (Pict.#7,P.23 ; some other forms below)

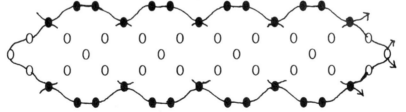

Alternate designs: 1) Use 3rd color on outside.
2) Different color for each inside cross.

8b. FOR A FANCIER EXPANDED DESIGN:

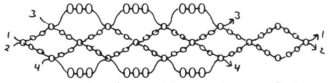

Edge unit can be 4 small beads or 3 larger ones.

8c. "BORDERED CROSSES" — LAKOTA STYLE:

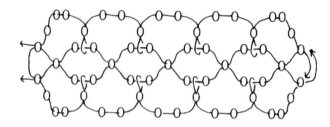

Make inside crosses first; come back on outside.

IV. PEYOTE WEAVE

Also called the "Gourd Stitch". This method of beading is reserved for religious or ritualistic articles by some of the southwestern Tribes as well as by the Cree of Canada. It is used for things connected with the Peyote ceremonies and dance accessories. One of my first Indian instructors warned me against giving offence in using this technique. The Lakota ladies in the Buechel Museum (Rosebud Res., So. Dakota) show great respect for all such things in their care. On the other hand, I have seen women as far apart as Winnebago and Taos making trinkets for sale using this weave. (Best rule - be respectful of other people's feelings - always.) I have found other differences in attitude concerning beads as, for instance, in the use and meaning of the "Spirit Bead" (intentional mistake) and again in the meanings attached by some to "Ghost Beads" (juniper-berries) while others wear them only as decoration. Such observations must underline the fact that we are uninformed when we think of Indians as a certain type of people when, in fact they are many kinds of people with different backgrounds and culture.

Back to beads: Among the Eastern Cherokee (North Carolina) all the beaded belts that I saw were made with the Peyote weave (13 bead wide) using large "Pony" beads. An example of this is shown in the front cover picture.

Peyote weaving can be in flat form (belts), tube form (necklaces, headbands) or used to cover irregularly shaped objects. The essential technique is in adding one bead at a time and then going back thru a previous bead while keeping the work tight. Also, there are variant forms such as "add one, back thru two". There is also a "Paiute" version (see Page 55) in which the beads are turned the other way.

The small Indian doll (see Page 54) often seen in souvenir stores is a "Peyote Tube".

The "Beaded Triangle" (see Page 63) is an example of the "Paiute" technique.

9.   PEYOTE TUBE:

(pictures; #9,P.23 & #3,P.39)
Start with a ring of beads (odd number 5-7-9-11), then add a 2nd row. This example is a 7-bead tube

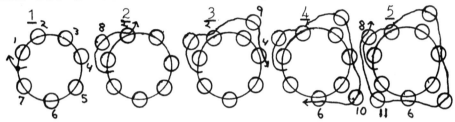

Fig.1 - String 7 beads and tie in a circle.
Fig.2 - Add bead #8 and BT (back thru) bead #2.
Fig.3 - Add #9 and BT #4.
Fig.4 - Add #10 and BT #6.
Fig.5 - Add #11 and BT #8.

Up to here it will lie flat on the surface. Now pull it up tight and it will be cup-shaped which will become a tube as you continue adding one bead at a time and "BT" the second old one.

Peyote fabric will take this appearance. (For circular stripes add rows in alternating colors)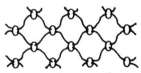

A number of interesting spirals can be made:
5-bead tube - adding in order ● O O ● O O ● O O
alternates one spiral of ● and two of O.
7-bead tube - adding alternate ● and O gives two spirals of each. Adding units of ● O O has same effect as in 5-bd. Units of ● O O O will give one spiral of ● and three of O. Try experimenting for other combinations (3 colors ?)

(28)

This interesting Peyote variation has double
beads in place of
singles in Peyote
tubes. This makes
a very attractive
key-ring drop. (Terri Brightnose, Cree)

10. PEYOTE FLAT

(picture; #1,P23)

This can be done either even or odd number of
beads wide. Even is easier to make as both edges
are the same. Odd works better if you want a
symmetrical design since it has a center line.

10a.   EVEN: (6-wide in this example - easily
adjusted to any other even number by adding even
number of beads to the original pickup)

Tie first bead on end of thread.
Pick up 6 more beads, #s 2 - 7,
(number added here equals width
of the resulting piece) "BT" (for back thru) #5,
add #8 , BT #3 , add #9 , BT #1.
Pull tight and it will look like ->
This is the base on which to work.

Continue back and forth adding one
new bead and "BT" second old bead.
both edges use the same turn around
by picking up first bead of the new row.

Variations of design can be worked out. Suggest
that you diagram the one you want so you can plan
the rows that will give that design. For example,
these eight rows (for 6-bead wide) repeated in
order, will give diagonals.
Have a base before starting the numbered rows -

Row 1. ● 0 0   3. ● ● 0   5. 0 ● ●   7. 0 0 ●
    2. 0 0 ●   4. 0 ● ●   6. ● ● 0   8. ● 0 0

10b.   UNEVEN: Make a 2-bead
loop.   Add beads for width of the
piece you want (here 9 added beads
will produce a 9-wide piece). Back
to the beginning adding beads a, b
& c while tying them to 7,5,3 & 1.
This finishes the first three rows
(R1,R2,R3). Add R4 & R5. The right
edge is same as in the "EVEN" pattern. Left edge
bead has a loop around the thread just above it.

R1 R2 R3 R4 R5 R6 R7 R8

11a.   FLOWER CLUSTER: (see picture #1, P.31
and #6, P.39)   Also called "Double Daisy"
(There are a number of ways to make this
pattern. This method is easier than the
one in my earlier books. I got it from a
long-time bead-weaving friend, Joyce Nasal)

It is a very attractive
basic peyote weave with
extra outside beads added.
Makes a nice choker by
itself or with some daisy-on-a-string (p.15)
tassels hung from the center sections of it.

Tie ● on thread. Add ● ● ● ●.
"BT"(back thru) #3.   Add ●.
"FT"(forward thru) #1.
Pull this base up tight to
     look like this -->

Continue adding Rows until
it is an inch or more long.
(a Row is once across the
work).   KEEP IT TIGHT
What you have now is a
"Flat Peyote - 4-wide"
     Make last Row (F - B), i.e., add (F) bead,
  BT , add (B) bead, FT , then start with Row 1.
Row 1 (B - F)

Row 2 (X - B)   B = background
Row 3 (B - F)
Row 4 (F - B)   F = flower color
Row 5 (F - B)
You now have this ->   X = center color

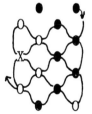

To finish the flower pick up three
"F" beads and circle back thru the
four "F" beads already in place.
Pull the circle of beads tight
and repeat the pattern starting
again with Row 1.

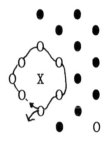

11b. "6-WIDE" FLOWER CLUSTER:

Base   Pull up to

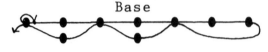

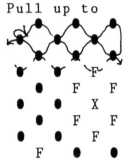

Row 1	●●F	Row 4	FF●
Row 2	FF●	Row 5	●●F
Row 3	●●X	Repeat	

For flowers further apart
add Row 6 ●●● & Row 7 ●●●

When done with larger beads
(pony or crow) this makes a beautiful lady's
belt (the belt is beautiful too)

11c. 6-WIDE 3-COLOR FLOWER CLUSTER:

cluster. Same base as "11b"

Rows:
	1.	●	1	●		●		1		●
	2.	●	1	1			1		1	●
	3.	1	2	1		1		2		1
	4.	●	2	2			2		2	●
	5.	1	3	1		1		3		1
	6.	●	2	2			2		2	●
	7.	1	2	1		1		2		1
	8.	●	1	1			1		1	●
	9.	●	1	●		●		1		●
	10.	●	●	●		●	●		●	
	11.	●	●	●		●	●		●	

Repeat Rows   (submitted by Ruth Fedors)

LOOP FASTENERS   for chokers and neck-laces.

Size 10/0 seed-beads and 1/4 in. Crow beads.
Can be used
in place of
clasps.

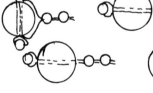

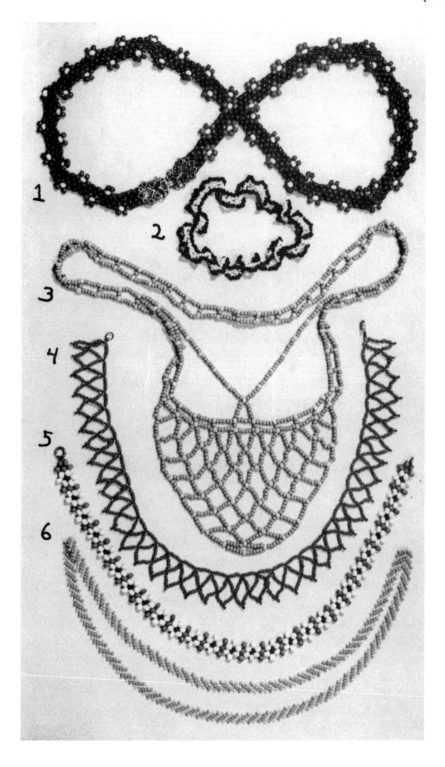

Bead-work by *Horace Goodhue*. The designs are: 1. "Flower Cluster" belt 2. "Ogalala Butterfly" 3. "Shoshone Web" 4. "Spider" choker, variant 5. "6-bead Daisy Bar" 6. "5-bead Diagonals" Photograph by *Terry Schwab*.

V. "FANCIES"

12a. LACY TUBE

I got this one from Claudia Wimett at the
"Things Unlimited" shop near Santa Fe, New Mexico
Tie 0 on thread, then add –

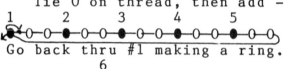

```
1     2     3     4     5
```

Go back thru #1 making a ring.

```
              6
Add   0 0 ● 0 0,   Go thru #3
Add   0 0 ● 0 0,   Go thru #5
Add   0 0 ● 0 0,   Go thru #6.
```

Pull up tight
to start tube
shape. Continue
by adding units
of 0 0 ● 0 0 and
back thru every second ● to make rectangles.

Interesting variations of this can be made by
substituting bugle beads.

12b. Base X ▱ X00X ▱ X00X ▱
Unit to add   00X ▱   -->

12c. Base 0 ▬ 0 ▱ 0 ▬ 0 ▱ 0 ▬
Unit to add   ▱ 0 ▬   -->

12d. Base 0 ▱ 000 ▱ 000 ▱
Unit to add   00:::   -->

12e. An advanced version of Lacy Tube on P.50, #5

13. INTERWEAVE:

A solid pattern –
but it takes a lot of time.
Start with top row string to full desired length

```
          2 3   1     4     5
```

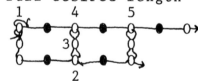

From bead #1 add 0 0 ● 0 0
and make a figure-8 thru #4
by going back thru #3 and
then forward thru bead #2

Step: Add ● 0 0   and make a figure-8 thru #5.
Repeat Steps adding ● 0 0   and making figure-8's.

The Interweave can be stretched out by adding a
number of ●'s
between the
figure-8's. 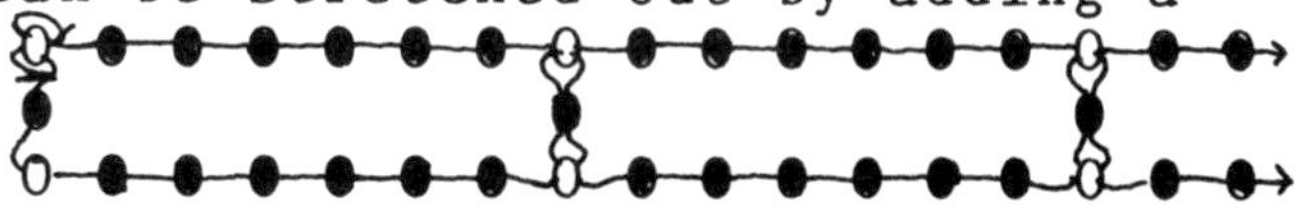
Picture #3,P.21   It looks something like a "6-3"
ladder but is much firmer.

14. **SPIDER**:   I got this one from Myrna Spears
(Ojibwa) at Red   1   2   3   4
Lake. Make the
baseline first
with double thread
for strength.If for
a choker,put clasps
on first.   We have   5   7
found it convenient
(but not necessary)
to stretch the baseline
across a loom for ease
in working. Now to add   6   9
webbing, start back at
#1. Add –   5   6
    ● ● ● ● 0 ● ● ● ● 0
and back thru 5 beads.
    Add ● ● ● ●,up thru #2.   8
    Add   ● ● ● ● 0 ● ● ● ●
and down thru #6.   Add
  ● ● ● ● 0 0 0 0 and BT #8
Pull it tight and add ● ● ● ● 0 ● ● ● ● , BT #7.
    Add   ● ● ● ● and up thru # 3 on the baseline.
Continue playing Spider up and down the webbing.
A single larger bead or a pearl drop can be
substituted for the three beads at the bottom.

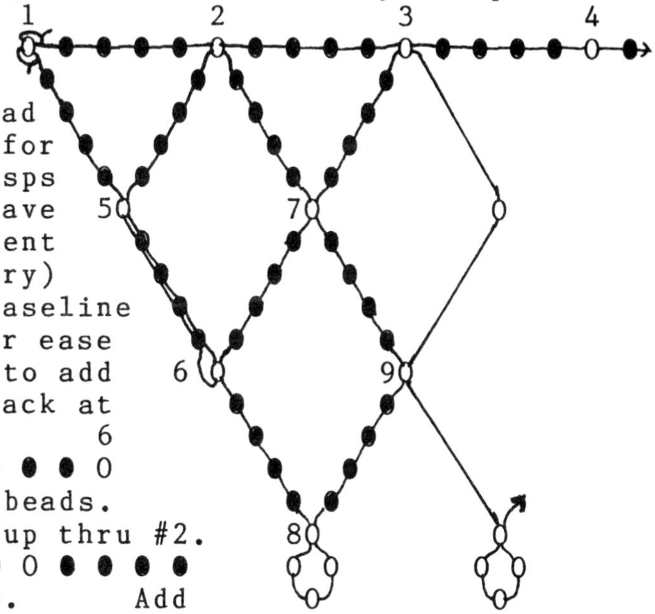

There are so many pretty variations of the Spider
style (especially in Navajo and Mohave country)
that I couldn't describe them all. However I'll
give some hints and you are on your own.

= – = – = – = – = – = – = – = – = – = – = – = – =

Room for a thought: "A mistake shows
                            that you're trying"

The fellow who made no errors
                    probably made no hits either.

SOME "SPIDER" IDEAS:

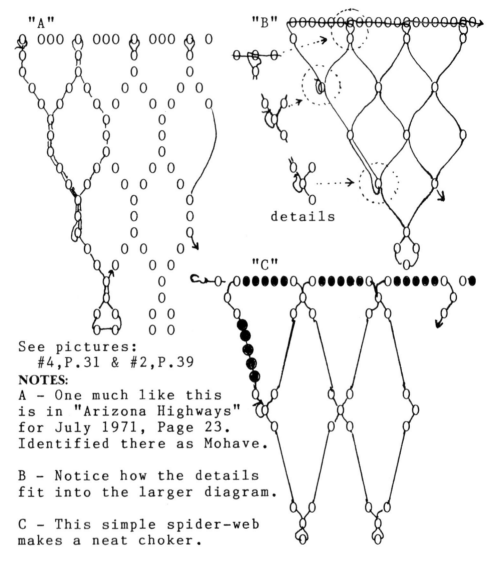

"A"

"B"

details

"C"

See pictures:
  #4,P.31 & #2,P.39

NOTES:

A - One much like this
is in "Arizona Highways"
for July 1971, Page 23.
Identified there as Mohave.

B - Notice how the details
fit into the larger diagram.

C - This simple spider-web
makes a neat choker.

I got A from a Museum piece, B from Linda Snow
(Seneca) and C from a Navajo lady in Taos.

For all of these I suggest making the baseline
first, using double thread. You will notice that
if there is an odd number of units going down
then the upper loop goes thru only one bead and
if the number is even then the upper loop goes
thru a whole unit on the baseline.

15. APACHE LEAF: I copied this from a choker I saw in a Museum in Phoenix.   ┌──(1 unit)──┐
Start with a baseline made   0 ● ● ● ● ● 0 ● ●
up in units as shown. 30 units (size 10/0 beads) make a 17-inch choker. When stringing base, omit last two beads from last unit. I recommend stretching the base across a loom for convenience while making the leaves - prevents tangles.

Each leaf is made in nine Steps.

1. At the starting point add 2 ●'s and 8 0's (use 3 ●'s instead of 2 in first leaf only) "TB" (by TB I mean "turn back" thru next bead on the thread)

2. Add 9 0's, go thru the middle ● on base line, "TB"

See Picture # 5 P.39

3. Add 2 0's, go thru first 3 0's of Step 1.
4. Add 0 ● 0, go thru beads 5 & 4 of Step 2.
      (Steps 4,5 & 6 will make a fig-8 thru center)
5. Add 1 0, go thru the ● of Step 4, add another 0, go thru 2nd & 3rd 0 of Step 1.
6. Thru 0 ● 0 of Step 4 and on thru #6 of Step 2.
7. Add 3 ●'s, go thru 0 on the baseline, "TB".
8. Add ● ● ● 0 and "TB".
9. Add 3 ●'s, go thru 0 on the baseline, "TB",.
                   REPEAT from Step 1.

= - = - = - = - = - = - = - = - = - = - = - = - =

16. SHOSHONE WEB: I copied this one from another Museum piece. It is good either as a choker or a bib. First make the complete base unit using any weave you wish. In the diagram I show the base as "6-bead dot" pattern #4a. Put on a clasp OR, as a loop, make it long enough to slip over the head.
 Now build the web on the base unit, making it as wide or narrow as you like. A good effect if the "corner" beads are larger than the "running beads. I made the one in the picture, Page 31, with #s 5 and 7 pony beads on "Interweave" base, #13.

With the neck piece completed, start at "1" and add ● ● ● O ● ● . Go thru "2". Add another such group of seven (or could use nines) beads and go thru "3". Continue the same until you have the width you want. To turn back, go thru the last four beads. Weave across the piece again and make the same turn there.

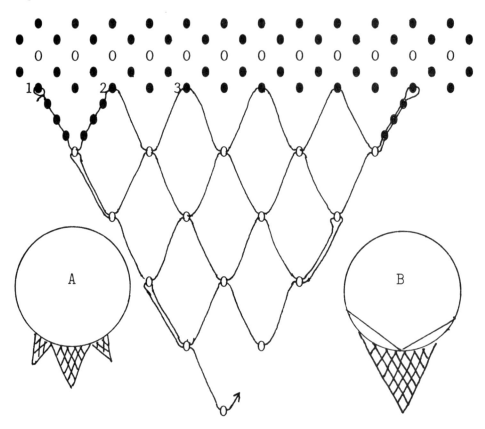

VARIATIONS: Combinations of webs can be made as in "A". If the web gets too heavy it may sag out of shape. Such trouble can be helped by cross-braces as shown in "B".

Let me remind you again, keep the work tight. That is the hallmark of good bead-craftsmanship. And don't worry about the mistakes that will inevitably turn up in your work - 'specially if you are doing it for fun rather than as an anxious chore. After all - you're a human bean - not a robot or a patent beading machine.

VI. "ZIG-ZAG" VARIATIONS

There are so many of these zig-zag patterns —
I have samples of thirty of them. Obviously I
won't discuss them all, but I will give some of
the better looking examples and then give a
mathematical analysis of them whereby you can,
with a little patience, work out any others that
you may want to use. I identify the zig-zags by
"code" numbers which I will explain later.

The "zig-zag" necklaces are fast and easy to
make. The thread routing is the
same in all of them.   Starting
from a certain "base" new beads
are added to the thread and then
are fastened down by putting the needle "back
thru" a bead (or beads) of the previous Step.
I use "BT" in my notes to represent this going
"back thru". The Steps are the same both ways.

The difference between the various patterns
is in how many new beads are added in each Step
and where the "BT" is made. You will find that
it goes faster if you turn the work over in your
hand after each Step - you are then working in
the same direction all the time.

Various fancy color effects are possible
even tho I am limited to just black and white
(● and O) here. Use your imagination and
experiment with other color combinations.

17.   "2-1-1":

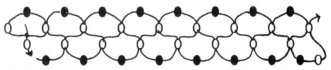

Base: Pick up O ● O, tie in a circle and add O.
Step: Add ● O and BT the second bead back along
the thread. Keep repeating the same Step.

18.   "3-1-1":

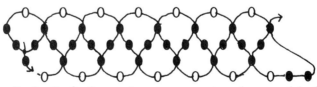

Picture
#6, P.23

Base: Pick up ● ● O ● ●, tie in a circle, add ●.
Step: Add O ● ●, BT the third bead back along the
thread. Repeat Step. This Z-Z looks better if the
O's are larger than the ●'s

19. "3-1-2":

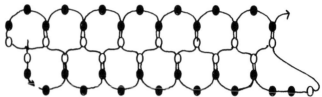

Base: Pick up 0 ● ● ● 0 , tie circle, add 0●.
Step: Add ● ● 0 , BT 3rd AND 4th beads.

20. "4-2-1":

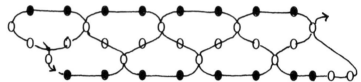

Base: Pick up 0 0 ● ● 0 0, tie circle, add 0.
Step: Add ● ● 0 0 , BT the third bead.

21. "5-2-1":

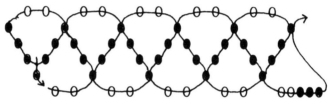

Base: Pick up ● ● ● 0 0 ● ● ●, tie circle, add ●.
Step: Add 0 0 ● ● ● , BT fourth bead on thread.

22. "6-3-1":

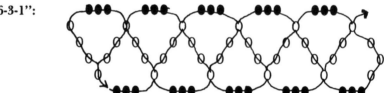

Base: Pick up 000 ●●● 000. Circle and add 0.
Step: Add ● ● ● 0 0 0, BT 4th bead on thread.

23. "7-4-1":

Base: Pick up ●●● 0000 ●●● . Circle. Add ● .
Step: Add 0000 ●●● and BT 4th bead.

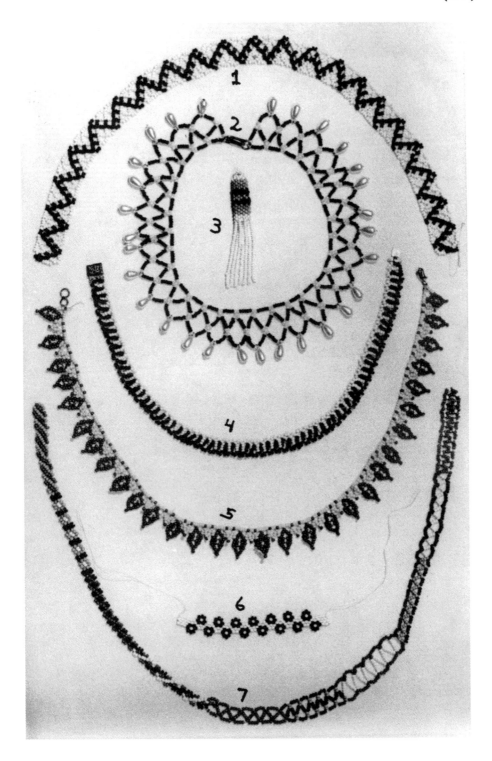

Bead-work by *Cecile Malack* and *Horace Goodhue*. The designs are: 1. "Double Zig-zag's" 2. "Spider" choker 3. "Peyote Tube" eardrop 4. "6-2-1" (Combs) choker 5. "Apache Leaf" choker 6. "Flower Cluster" 7. Various "Zig-zag" samples. Photograph by *Terry Schwab*.

(40)

24. "7-3-2":

A nice one !

Base: Pick up 0000 ●●● 0000. Circle and add 0 0.
Step: Add ●●● 0000 and BT 5th AND 6th.

25. "5-3-1": Now let's try one with a little
design in it.

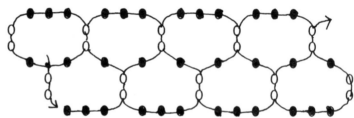

Base: 0 ● ● ● ● 0 0, tie in circle, add 0 .
Step 1: ● ● ● ● ● ● , BT 3rd
     2: 0 0 0 0 ● , BT 3rd   Deb Gilbertson
     3: 0 0 0 0 0 , BT 3rd   worked this out
     4. ● ● ● ● 0 , BT 3rd

26. "6-3-2":

Base: ● 0 0 ● ● ● 0 0 ● , tie circle , add 0 0.
Step: ● ● ● 0 0 0 ● and BT 4th AND 5th.

27. "4-1-2":

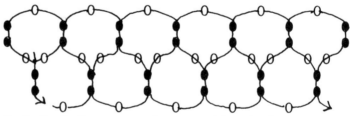

Base: 0 ● ● 0 ● ● 0 , circle , add ● ● .
Step: 0 ● ● 0 and BT 4th AND 5th.

INTERMISSION! In these notes I am not trying to make the patterns look attractive – rather I am using such combinations as will show the details of the patterns most clearly. To show what I mean I will draw the next pattern in two different ways. There is one local beader selling necklaces thru the boutiques who seems to have just one favorite pattern (the "Double Zig-zag #35). Yet she uses such a variety of color effects that one has to look carefully at the pieces to see that the pattern is exactly the same in the different looking designs.

   With that in mind I want to encourage all of my readers who are really "into" beading, whether for hobby interest or for sale, to experiment freely with new color combinations in any of these patterns.   Have fun being original !

28a. "5-2-2": Routine two-color diagram would be

Can you
work out
your own
Base and
Step ?

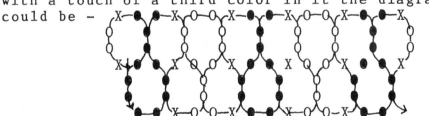

28b. Now if we want a more attractive design with a touch of a third color in it the diagram could be –

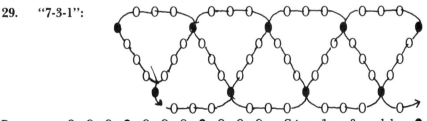

   Use my book to learn new patterns but then be on your own in making good designs with them.

29. "7-3-1":

Base: 0 0 0 ● 0 0 0 ● 0 0 0. Circle & add ● .
Step: 0 0 0 ● 0 0 0.   BT 5th.

(42)

30. "8-4-1":

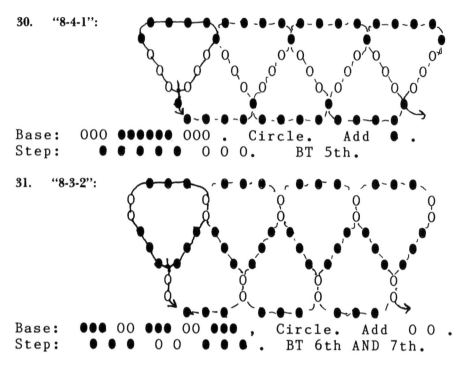

Base: 000 ●●●●●● 000 . Circle.   Add ● .
Step: ● ● ● ● ● ● O O O.   BT 5th.

31. "8-3-2":

Base: ●●● OO ●●● OO ●●● , Circle. Add O O .
Step: ● ● ● O O ● ● ● .   BT 6th AND 7th.

32. "12-4-4":   Picture #3, page 11. This pattern
has been a class favorite (in red and white).
We make it as a long necklace with ends fastened
together with a ladder stitch.

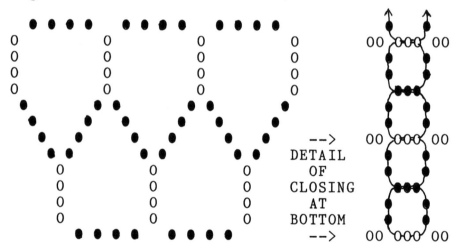

-->
DETAIL
OF
CLOSING
AT
BOTTOM
-->

       Tassel attachment shown in picture
Base: 4 ●'s, 4 O's, 4 ●'s, 4 O's, 4 ●'s. Add 4 O's
Step: 4 ●'s, 4 O's, 4●'s.   BT third set of 4(O's).
     The first time I saw this pattern it was being
worn by an Ogalala man, Pine Ridge, South Dakota.

33. "6-2-1": Two designs using this pattern.

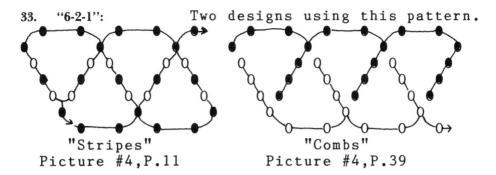

"Stripes"
Picture #4,P.11

"Combs"
Picture #4,P.39

As a test of your understanding of the explanations I have given in this section (or perhaps as a test of my explanations) I suggest that you try to work out your own keys for the two variations of the preceding "6-2-1" pattern. You will notice that "Stripes" needs only one step while "Combs" requires two steps.

Now for my promised analysis of the "Zig-zags" as a class of patterns. As you have noted, the back and forth movement of the thread is the same in all of them.

There are THREE variables involved: A) the number of beads picked up before going "back thru"; B) the number of beads on the outside of each unit; and C) the number of beads the needle goes back thru. Since these three variables determine the pattern, let's call that pattern by the code name, "A-B-C".

Thus the code name of the last one, "6-2-1", describes that pattern and that pattern only since it shows that SIX (A) new beads are picked up before the thread goes back thru that ONE (C) bead which leaves TWO (B) others on the outside.

If you didn't take up my challange to work out your own keys for "6-2-1" before, why not go back and try it now. You will find it easy to do. If all the loops of a pattern are the same you will find that only one step is needed. The fancier ones will need more. For instance, #28b, "5-2-2", takes six steps. Knowing the above you will be able to classify any zig-zag pattern that you see and reproduce it more easily.

VII.   FANCY ZIG-ZAGS

These patterns, zig-zag in nature, do not have the thread routing discussed before.

34a.   POINTED ZIG-ZAG:

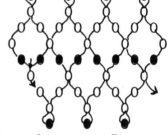

Base: Pick up ● 0 0 0 ● and "TB" (meaning turn back thru next to the last bead) Add 0 0 ● . Tie.   Add 0.
  Step 1: Add   0 0 ● . "TB" Pull it up tight.
  Step 2: Add   0 0 ● , then go ACROSS the work and thru the first bead BEYOND the center line.   Repeat.
  (to tighten up Step 1 hold outside bead between your fingernails and pull out on the thread)

34b.   POINTED Z-Z VARIANT:

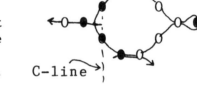

Base: Made the same way as previous pattern except for the extra beads.   The diagram shows a completed base.   A real neat design.   C-line
  Step 1: Add 0 0 ● . "TB".
  Step 2: Add 0 0 ● ● . Go across the center and thru 1st AND 2nd beads BEYOND the center line.

35.   DOUBLE ZIG-ZAG: **35a.   BASIC DESIGN:**

If you like making up new color effects this is a good pattern to work with.   There are many possible variations from the basic design but you should use the basic until you are sure of it.

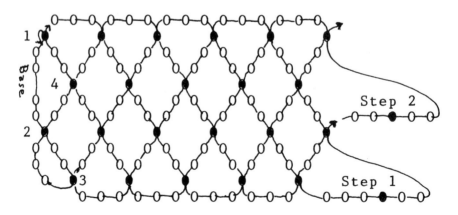

Base: Tie # 1 bead on end of thread and add
eleven more beads as
shown and go back
thru bead # 2. Add
0 0 ● 0 0 and back thru # 1. Pull it up tight
and this is how the
base should look now -->

Step 1: Add 0 0 0 ● 0 0. Back thru 4th bead (#4).
Step 2: Add 0 0 ● 0 0. Forward (across the work)
thru the 6th bead (#3) in the diagram. Repeat.

Now I will suggest several nice variations
for you to try after you are familiar with the
thread routing. I will give you an idea of how
they will look but will omit details.

35b. SNAKE DESIGN — TWO COLOR: (Pictures, P23 & 39)
Base: (see diagram)

Step 1: 0 0 0 ● ● ●. Turn back thru 4th bead
2: ● ● 0 0 0. Then go
forward thru the 6th
3: 0 0 0 0 0 0   BT 4th
4. 0 0 ● ● ●   FT 6th
5. ● ● 0 0 ● ●   BT 4th
6. ● ● ● 0 0   FT 6th

35c. SNAKE — THREE COLOR:
Base: (see diagram)
S1. 0 0 0 ● ● ●   BT 4th
2: X X ● ● ●   FT 6th
3. 0 0 0 0 0 0   BT 4th
4. ● ● ● X X   FT 6th
5. ● ● ● X X   BT 4th
6. ● ● ● 0 0   FT 6th

35d. "WAVY": (from Karen Swan, Lakota artist)
4-color (Edging, Center line, Points, Filler)
Base: (see diagram)
S1. E E E P P P   BT 4th
2. F F C C C   FT 6th
3. E E E P F F   BT 4th
4. C C C F F   FT 6th
5. E E E C C C   BT 4th
6. F F P P P   FT 6th

35e. CENTER LINE — THREE COLOR: <●>black,<R>red,
<G>green.   Use this base, then the Steps

Step 1 ●●●●RR , BT 4th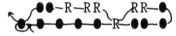
Step 2 GGGRR , FT 6th
   Repeat this Row (St.1 & 2)

35f. BRAID — THREE COLOR:
Base (see diagram)
   Row 1 ●●●G●● , BT#4 - ●●RRR , FT#6
   Row 2 RRR●RR ,   "   - RRGGG ,   "
   Row 3 GGGRGG ,   "   - GG●●● ,   "
      Repeat the Rows

35g. HEARTS (VALENTINE FAVORITE):
        Base as shown,
        then the Rows

Row 1 ●●●RRR - ●●RRR
Row 2 ●●●●RR - ●●RRR   < For solid red heart: >
Row 3 ●●●●●● - RRRRR   < Row 1 ●●●RRR - RRRRR >
Row 4 ●●●●●● - ●●R●●   < ROW 2 ●●●●RR - RRRRR >
Row 5 ●●●●RR - RRR●●   < Rows 3,4,5 as given >

    Repeat and here is what you get -

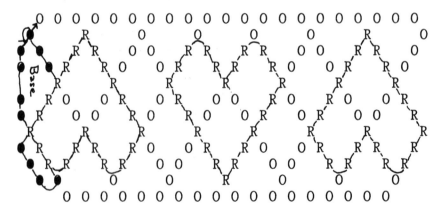

To have the hearts in same direction, make this
    change in base and
    then use these Rows
    (from John Ucko)
   Row 1 ●●●●RR-RRR●●   Row 4 ●●●●●●-RRRRR
   Row 2 ●●●RRR-RRRRR   Row 5 ●●●●●●-●●●●●
   Row 3 ●●●●RR-RRRRR   Row 6 ●●●●●●-●●R●●

36. RED LAKE ZIG-ZAG:

This was given to me by an Ojibwa friend while I was visiting her bead class at the Red Lake (Minnesota) High School. She called it "Grandmother's pattern". The next time I saw it was at the "Wrangler" store in Cheyenne where the clerk called it Navajo work. I have also heard it called Canadian Cree. Whereever it came from, it's an interesting pattern.

The same friend gave me the key to it after I had shown her class some patterns unknown there. That is how I have obtained most of my patterns - trading knowledge with Indian beaders all over the country.   It has been great fun !

36a. 8-BEAD DIAGONAL — TWO-COLOR:

1 2 3 4 5 6 7

Base: Tie first bead on thread. Add #2 thru #7. BT #1. Add 8,9, and X (000). BT the 4th (original 5). It's very important to keep work tight with this pattern.

Step 1. 0 0 ● ● ● BT 2nd (#X)
     2.   0 0 0   BT 4th
     3. ● ● 0 0 0 BT 2nd   BASE
     4.   ● ● ●   BT 4th

BASE
2—3—4
1—7—6—5
8—9—X

("BT 2nd" means turn back over the last bead and go thru the next one - i.e., the second bead back along the thread)
("BT 4th" means turn back along the thread. Skip the first 3 you come to and go thru the 4th one)

36b. 8-BEAD DIAGONAL — MULTIPLE COLORS

(1, 2, 3, etc. represent consecutive new colors)
Base: Pick up 2-1-1-1-2-2-2. BT 1st bead. Tighten.

1—1—1
2—2—2—2

1 1 1
2 2 2
3—3—3
2→

1 1 1
2 2 2 2—2-2
3 3 3—3—3—3

1 1 1
2 2 2 2 2 2
3 3 3 3 3 3→
4—4—4

Base   Step 1   Step 2   Step 3

Forward step 1: 3 3 3 (new color). BT 4th bead.
 Return step 2: 2 2 3 3 3 (Two of previous color and three of this new color),   BT 2nd.

Continue alternating forward and return steps.
For. step 3: 4 4 4   BT 4th
Ret. step 4: 3 3 4 4 4   BT 2nd   And so on until
For. step 5: 5 5 5   BT 4th   you want to
Ret. step 6: 4 4 5 5 5. BT 2nd   repeat colors.

36c. DAISY-&-DOUBLE BAR — THREE -COLOR: A heavier and firmer pattern than the Daisy-Bar shown in #4b.

Base: 1 2 3 4 5 6 7, BT #1, Add 8 9 X, BT #5.
● ● ● ● ● C C   ● ● ●

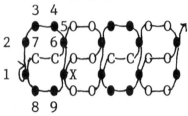

Ret. St.1: 00●00, BT 2nd

For. St.2: 0 0 ●, BT 4th

Ret. St.3: ●●●CC, BT 2nd

For. St.4: ● ● ●, BT 4th   Repeat the 4 Steps.

37. "POTAWATOMI WEAVE":

I was introduced to this pattern by fellow bead-teacher, Steve Chapman (Ojibwa).   It can be used to make any of the 6-bead designs shown under #4. This method is faster, once you have mastered it, as you pick up five beads at a time. With these three figures I hope to make it understandable to any beader.

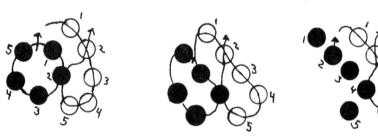

Figure 1. Base circle and pickup for Step 1.
Figure 2. Same after thread is pulled up tight.
Figure 3. Shows relation of any Step (the 0's)
           to its preceeding Step (the ●'s).
To put into a Rule we may say   –
   "For each Step: Add 5 new beads. Go BACKWARD
   thru the front bead, #4, of the preceeding
   Step. Then go BACKWARD thru the second bead
   of this Step. Pull up tight."
The easiest way to get a 5-bead multi-color
   diagonal is, "Base, 22112. Pick up four of a
   new color, then one of the last color,33332".
Ending: To end this pattern neatly at any point
   just add the first two beads of the next Step
   and down, not up, thru the previous #4 bead.

37a.   WINNEBAGO DESIGN: We have had this before but now we can make it using this new method. The colors are Red, Black and Yellow. The diagram is drawn to show the Base and Steps separately.

```
   Base: Y R R R R              STEPS
Step 1: R R R B B        1    2    3    4    5    6
     2: B B B Y Y       ⌐R╲ ⌐B╲ ⌐Y╲ ⌐Y╲ ⌐Y╲ ⌐B╲
     3: Y Y B Y Y      R↑  R   B   Y   Y   B   R
     4: Y Y B B Y       ╲Y↑ R↑ B↑ B↑ B↑ R↑ ╲
     5: Y B R R B      R   R   B   Y   Y   B   R
     6: B R Y R R       ╲R╱ ╲B╱ ╲Y╱ ╲Y╱ ╲Y╱ ╲B╱ End
```

37b.   The 6-bead daisies (see page 15) can also be made using this pattern.

4a. Dots: Base ● 0 0 0 0. Repeat step 0 0 ● 0 0.

4b. Circle-bar: Base X 0 0 0 0 and two steps.
            1: 0 0 ● 0 ●   2: ● 0 X 0 0

4c. Diagonals: Base ● ● 0 0 ● and two steps.
            1: 0 0 0 0 ●   2: ● ● ● ● 0

38.   "PANSY":   A pretty necklace from Arizona. In construction it is a fancy ladder (see P.22) I like it with alternating white and navy blue flowers with red and white pearl center beads.

Use a larger bead for "X" Two needles, one at each end of your thread. Pick up 2 beads for the base. Now do Step 1. Add 6 beads to each side and CROSS needles thru the X bead. Step 2. Run needles forward thru next 3 OLD BEADS to the "a" points.

Step 3. ADD 11 to each side. CROSS them thru "X".
Step 4. Run needles thru 3 OLD BEADS to points "b"
Step 5. ADD 3 to each side. CROSS thru 2 NEW BEADS Back to Step 1. to continue.(New color if desired)
VARIATION: To put circles between flowers add --
Step 6. ADD 6 to each side,CROSS thru 2 new beads.
For EARDROPS : Use first 5 Steps then add 3 beads to each side for the wire.   (from Mary Kimball)

They didn't find a
place in the book but they are worth knowing.

----

1) For a more lacy "D-ZZ" use this base with
8 & 7 beads in Steps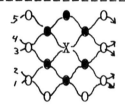

Step 1 00000●000 , BT#5
Step 2 0000●000 , FT#8
   This gives the basic dot pattern but
   you can change it to your own pattern.

----

2) "Finger-rings":   I am sometimes asked what
is a good pattern for making rings.   There are
several that will work out well.
   1. Bordered crosses (#8) is easy to do but
you must note that it gets a bit shorter when
you add the outside ● ●'s.
   2. Interweave (#13) starting with a single
string ring as a base.
   3. Zig-zags "2-1-1" (#17) or "3-1-1" (#18).
ZZ rings look good but are hard to tie together.

----

3)   A "flower" can
       be placed on a
       Peyote tube or
       flat in five
       consecutive
       rows.

----

4) Orpha's Red-White-Blue design for her belt
and necklace.   (Page 38, #21, "5-2-1")
       Base: W W B B B B W W, Circle & add R
       Step 1: R R R W W, "BT" 4th bead
       Step 2: B B B W W, "   " : Repeat.

----

5) "Pin-wheel" on a Lacy Tube. (#12. Page 32)
       At intervals (1" or more) stop the forward
movement and go once around the tube adding
outside points. Being attached to the "x" beads,
these will stand
out from the tube.

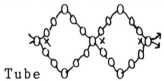

Tube

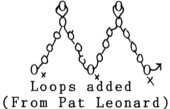

Loops added
(From Pat Leonard)

39.   NAVAJO NET

This interesting expansion of the double zig-zag has various other names (i.e., "Wide-web"). Tourists bring back beautiful samples of it from Mexico and from Morocco (North Africa).

Step 1 of the D-ZZ has 4 beads and then Step 2 (and as many more Steps as desired) have 3 beads each to the desired width.

You may have to plot it on paper first to get the color pick-up plan for the design you want.

One attractive 4-step pattern takes this base:

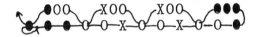

Then use these rows --

	St.1	St.2	St.3	St.4
	BT#3	FT#4	FT#4	FT#4
Row 1	●●00	X00	X00	●●●
Row 2	●●●●	●00	X00	X00
Row 3	●●●●	00X	00X	00●

Back to Row 1 and repeat.

You get -

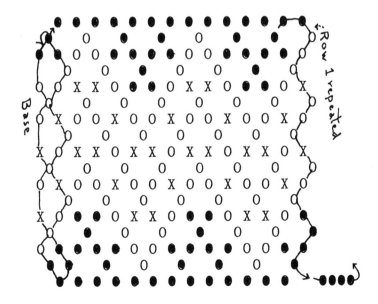

40. LAKOTA CHAIN

From a pattern in the Buechel Memorial Museum, St.Francis, Rosebud Reservation, South Dakota. It, like the "Red Lake ZZ", is a non-symmetrical ZZ as the foward and back steps are different. Makes a strong solid chain

1st DESIGN:
Solid color

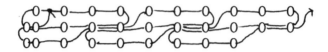

Base: Tie 000 in a circle,
     Add 000000 , BT 00

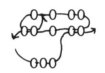

Step 1 Add 000 , forward
thru 2nd & 3rd of 6-loop

Step 2 Add 000000, back   0 0 00
     thru same two beads   00 0
                                 000

2nd DESIGN: Spiral 4-color, ("1","2",&"3" are
   Diagonals, "4" is a filler)
Base 122-tie circle - 433222 - back thru the
       22 of the first three.
Row 1 (Steps 1 & 2) 3 3 3 - 4 1 1 3 3 3
Row 2 (steps 3 & 4) 1 1 1 - 4 2 2 1 1 1
Row 3 (Steps 5 & 6) 222 - 433222, Repeat R.1

3rd DESIGN: Raindrops, 3-color (0 & X are
   drops, ● is filler)   Base ●●● - ●XX●●●
Row 1   X X X   -   X X X X X X
Row 2   X X X   -   ● 0 0 ● ● X
Row 3   0 0 0   -   0 0 0 0 0 0
Row 4   0 0 0   -   ● X X ● ● 0 , Repeat Rows.

41. THREE ROW: (from necklace at Berman Buckskin booth, MN St. Fair '75) Another non-sym. ZZ.

3-color: <●> black, <R> red, <T> turquoise

Base   R—R——●●TTT●●—R—R
             ●●TTT●●

Step 1 ●●●● RR ●● , "BT" TTT
Step 2 ●● RR ●●●● , BT RR ●●●●
Step 3 ●● TTT ●● , BT RR

Detail

Base

St.2   2   St.3   St.1

= - = - = - = - = - = - = - = - = - = - = - = - = - =

42. BRAIDS: "Flat" or "round" in contrasting colors are easy to make and are very attractive (have beads on strong thread)

Try this FLAT 3-STRAND with multiple strings. It is type"1-2-2".   "1-2-3" and "1-1-3" also work quite well

= - = - = - = - = - = - = - = - =

ROUND 4-STRAND: Tie strings together at one end and hook on a nail or pin and then hold two in each hand as in Fig.<1>
Step 1: Pass #4 down and under #3 & #2, then up and back over #2 to your right hand, Fig<2>
Step 2: Pass #1 down and under #2 & #4, then up and back over #4 to end as Fig.<3>. Repeat.
   RULE: "Down and under two, up and over one"
   <1>   <2>   <3>

VIII.   DOLLS

43.   INDIAN DOLL: This is made with the
Peyote Weave (11-bead tube). Most of the bead
dolls you see in the souvenir shops are made of
either 10/0 or 11/0 size seed beads altho I have
seen them made of #5 pony beads.
     Start with a circle of 11 red beads (which
becomes the belt-line of the finished doll.
Build upward with lines as numbered below. By
working up you can more easily compare the work
with the directions as you go along. Each line
will start at the middle of the back.
     Color code: 'R'ed,'W'hite,'B'lack,'P'ink.

```
5  W W W W W      10    B P P P B      16    B B B B B
4   W B W B W      9   B B P P B B     15   B B B B B B
3  W W W W W      8    B P R P B      14    B B P B B
2   W B W B W      7   W B P P B W     13   B B P P B B
1  W W W W W      6    W B P B W      12    B P P P B
                                      11   B B B B B B
```

Close top of the head with additional black
beads — see diagram. Pull the thread tight and
work it down into the body for attaching the arms.

     Arms: Attach them to the front side of 2nd
and 5th "W's" of lines 3 and 5.   String
W W W W P P P and thread back thru the "W's".
The "P's" will form a triangle representing hands.

     Legs: Two methods (easy and hard). The easy
way is to continue down with one tube using
colored beads and two vertical rows of black
(front and back) to indicate leg separation.
For separate legs add 3 lines down from the belt
(6,5,6 beads each) and then split into two 7-bead
tubes by adding three additional beads (see
diagram) across the center of the 11-bead tube.
Optional color for the legs. For the feet have
the last 14 beads of another color.

     Head-dress: Red (●) and white (O).
Attach front seven feathers to the first row of
the hair beads; the other two feathers to the
second row from the face. See details in diagram.

44. PAIUTE WEAVE:

This doll construction is the common Tube
Peyote weave, however, as mentioned before (P.27)
there is another Peyote weave which I have heard
called the "Paiute" version. In it the beads are
turned another way, as
shown in this diagram.

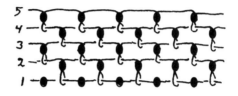

Since it is easy to
change number of beads
from row to row, it is
useful in covering an
irregular object.
(I learned this from a doll bootee). In order to
get the spacing right it shouldn't be sewed onto
a base until the second row is on. The "Paiute"
technique is used for the bead triangle (P.63).

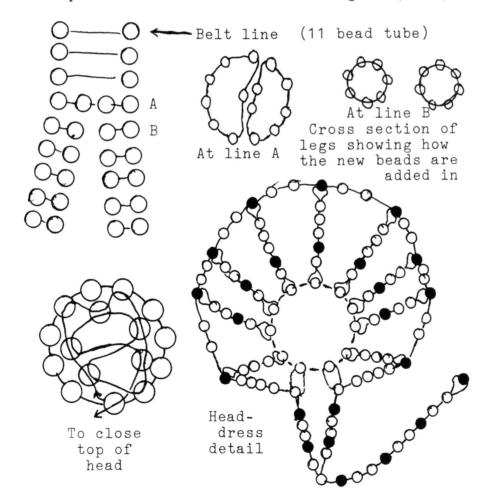

Belt line   (11 bead tube)

At line A

At line B
Cross section of
legs showing how
the new beads are
added in

To close
top of
head

Head-
dress
detail

45. LADY DOLL:

Use the same base and 16 lines of body-beads as shown for Indian man. Add line 17 (BBBBBB) Close top of head and put on arms (see diagrams).

Hat: Attach to the original line 15 & 16

Skirt: Add two lines below the belt-line (11 beads) & use them as the inside ring of the skirt. (note that only 9 of the 11 are needed for the skirt)

Legs:Attach to inside of belt-line. Top 3 beads of legs can be same size used in the body, but others will be of a larger size.

Colors: Optional. Hat & skirt look nice if mainly white with red for the corner beads. ("corner" beads are those with more than one thread thru them)

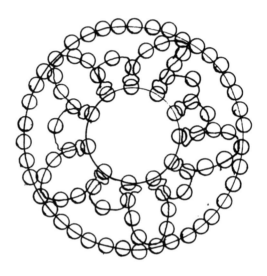

LADY DOLL'S HAT: inside ring are the original beads of lines 15 & 16.

←Beltline

LEGS

LADY
DOLL
SKIRT

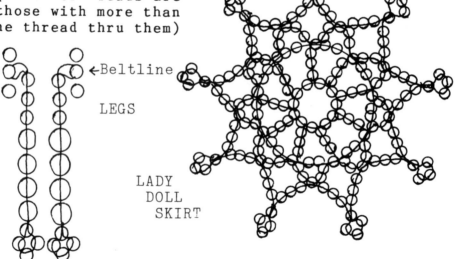

HELPFUL HINTS

KNOTS: Work usually starts with "Tie on a bead"
or "Tie in a circle". Do NOT tie a knot
in the thread itself. If you do then one
of two things will happen (both bad !).
 Either the next bead will slip over and
off or the knot will jam the bead so the
next thread can't go thru. Tie it around
the bead as shown. In tying use a square
knot. Be sure you don't make a "granny"
knot. I am naturally distrustful of nylon knots
so I always add a second knot over the first one.

NEW THREAD: To start a new thread while working,
I run the old thread back into the
piece and pull it out between two
beads. I start the new thread between the same two beads and work
it forward until I am at the place
where I am to continue the beading.
 Then I tie the two ends together,
cut off the "pig-tails" and by pulling the new thread tight the knot will usually
go down out of sight between the two beads.

DOUBLE-FIGURE-8-KNOT for ending a piece of work.

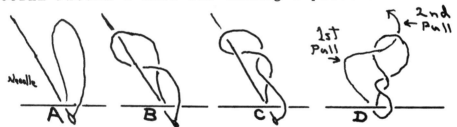

Run the thread back into the work and under some
firm crossing thread (Fig.A). At this point many
beaders use the simple sewing "figure-8" knot
(Fig.B) and pull it up tight. This is good but
sometimes slips out so I prefer to use a "double-
fig.8" (Fig.C) by giving the loop an extra half-
twist, then over the needle. The only trouble
with this knot is that sometimes it will "set"
before all the slack is out of it when you pull
out on the needle thread. To prevent this you
pull the thread BACK of the loop (Fig.D) tight,
taking up all the slack, and then "set" the knot
by pulling the needle thread out tight.
 I know it looks complicated but with a
little practice you will have a good solid knot.

LOOM WEAVING

Since there are many good instructions for looming in other books I did not cover it in my previous editions but, in response to my readers' requests, here it is. First is the loom itself:

Most beaders are more satisfied with their homemade looms than with those now available at craft stores because most commercial ones have wire frames which flex while you are stringing them making it very hard to get even tension on the strings (therefore; uneven work).

With nails or screws, fasten three pieces of wood together (Fig.A). The base should be three inches longer than the longest work you will do on it. 3 inches wide will handle most of the work you will do.

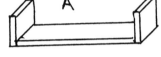

The ends should be about 3 inches high. Drive nails (spaced 1 in) in each end to hold your strings. If you want it stronger you can add cleats as in Fig. B and it is ready for stringing (Fig.C).

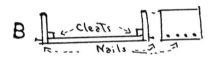

Run the strings (these are called the "warp") over the top from nail to nail while keeping them tight enough to 'zing' a little.   Place one more string than the number of beads-wide

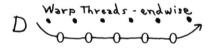

When weaving a wide piece, doubling the outside strings gives more strength.

Pick up your first row of beads and hold them UNDER the warp (Fig.D) and then push them UP to fit between the warp strings.   Holding the beads in place with a finger

pass your needle through the same beads back again so the 2nd string goes ABOVE the warp (Fig.E).   Tie a knot in the string and you have the first row finished. (These strings are called "weft" and this method of weaving is called "Double-Weft")

See suggestions below about selvage before
starting second row. Then add the second and
other rows in the same way (but with no knots).
    Warning: If you force the rows too tightly
together some beads will 'bubble up' when you
take the piece off the loom.

NEW THREAD: When your
thread gets too short, turn
it back into the work for 3
or 4 rows (Fig.F)and cut it
off – friction will hold it
securely; no knot is needed.
    Start the new thread back
several rows in the same way and work it up to
the starting place. You should use a different
set of beads so that they are not overloaded.

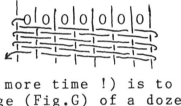

ENDING: Two ways; tape or
selvage.   A thin first aid
tape is better than masking
tape (which is apt to slip
off particularly if it gets
wet). The better way (takes more time !) is to
weave an over-&-under selvage (Fig.G) of a dozen
or so threads, which can be
turned under when you mount
the piece. To prevent slip-
page (in either method) tie
the warp ends before cutting them off (Fig.H).
Make these knots double for sake of security.

PATTERNS: Two ways again; graph or code.
Plot the design on beading graph paper and use
it as a guide to row-by-row pick-up. (The design
is distorted if you use squared graph paper.)
    For coding, make a list of the rows.
Example: (in making a red, white & blue piece)
    "Row 5: 3W-2R-1B-7R-2W". You will find coding
is easier if the design is large or complicated.

    Mounting on leather (suede/buckskin)
Ends: Turn selvage under and sew down
the strings between the beads
(all spaces or every 2nd one)
as in Fig.J.   Sides: using a
spiral stitch, sew down every 2nd or 3rd space.

CAUTION: When looming, throw away all under-size, oversize and odd-shaped beads (over your left shoulder for luck !). A few of them can spoil the looks of your whole work. If you are left-handed (as I am) you can reverse Figures D, E,F and G for easier working.

There are many other details in looming that you will learn by practice. I will add a few suggestions here. At the beginning you should also have a selvage as shown in Fig.G. Do not make it before the first row as you may not get the spacing right but if you add it right after the first row it will save the trouble of coming back later with another thread. In making a long piece you might want to start it from the middle of the design so as to get the two halves of equal length.

Rubbing beeswax along the warp after string-ing makes it stronger and may prevent splitting it with the needle on the return pass. If the piece will be long and subject to strain (as a belt or guitar strap) you may want to use a stronger warp thread ("Nymo" size "DD") and, if the leather you're using is soft and stretchy, baste a strip of heavy cloth or canvas to your leather before sewing on the bead strip.

Some loom instructions suggest notches on the top edge. I find them unnecessary if the strings have proper tension and, in any case, notches have no purpose after the first row is on.

If your work "bubbles up" when removed from the loom, pat it out lengthwise; it may get 1/4 inch longer but it will lie flat. If a bead binds at all when passing the needle through it, discard it as it will make trouble when you try to pass it again.

If you have an extra bead in your work, break it off by pushing a too-large needle into it. When you cut the piece off the loom leave the warp ends 3 or 4 inches long to make it easier to tie the selvage.

A wide belt has a tendency to fold in sidewise.
To prevent this, instead of using a heavy leather
base, I push a heavy leather liner into the
envelope formed when I have sewed down one end
and both sides of the bead piece and then sew
down the other end.

This "Double-Weft" method is not the only one
used by Indians but it is the most common one.
And this type of loom is not the only one either:
for extra wide or extra
long work a box- (or
window-) frame is some-
times used (Fig.K). If
the warp is wound all
way around it a result-
ing piece can be twice
the frame-length by slip-
ping it around the frame.

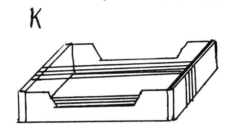

I suggest to my beginning beaders that they
use authentic Indian designs in looming rather
than trying to be original. We are, after all,
studying a Native Nations' culture and we have
no right to distort it. The best source of
designs I know of is the 12 pages of colored
graphs in "American Indian Beadwork", 1951, by
Hunt & Burshears. This book was out-of-print for
quite a while but is now available in paperback
    (published by Collier Books, NY, 1971).

Now begin looming: With patience and practice
you will be a skilled loom weaver. You'll like it.

Beginners' loom project (on headband or bracelet)
```
   Row-----1234567
        0000000000000000////000000000000000
        0000000000000000/X/0000000000000000
        0000///////////////////////////0000
        000000//XXXXXX/////XXXXXX//000000
        00000000//XXX//0///0//XXX//00000000
        0000000000///00//0//00///0000000000
        00000000000000///0////00000000000000
```
Code:Row 1   20-X-40   Row 4   20-2X-30
     Row 2   20-X-40   Row 5   20-/-X-/-20
     Row 3   20-2X-30   Row 6   20-/-X-/-20
                                      ,etc.

(62)

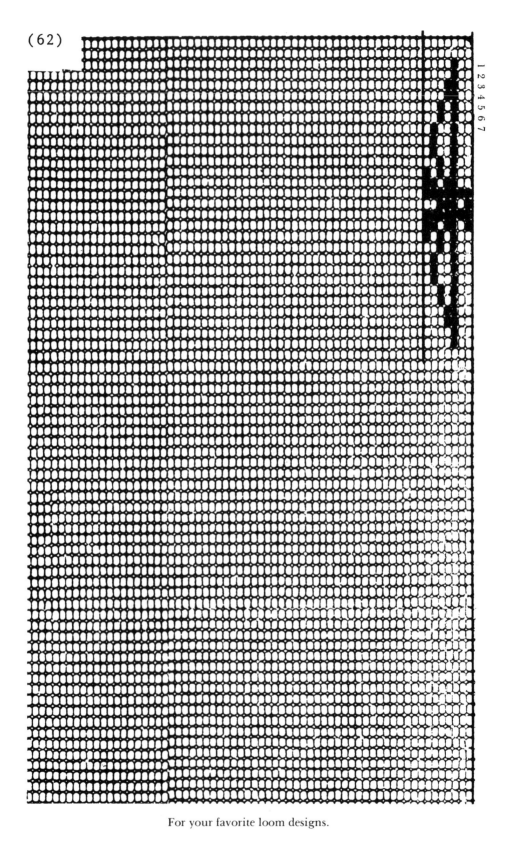

For your favorite loom designs.

TRIANGLE BASE

A very popular type of eardrop is
built on a solid triangle of beads. In a larger
form the same triangle can be used for pendants.
This uses the "Paiute" weave, somewhat like the
Peyote except that the beads are vertical, not
horizontal. It is explained on Page 55.

To start it, you make a base line of bugle beads
(they are small glass tubes quarter inch long or
less and same diameter as your beads). I usually
use 9 or 11 beads but I suggest that you start
with six for your first piece.

Start with a four-
foot thread - it
may be too much
but too long is
better than too
short !   Put a
needle on each end of it

  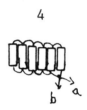

and string one bugle (see Fig. 1.) Now run both
ends of the thread thru a second bugle (Fig.2.).

Pull the thread down snug and add a third bugle
(Figure 3.). Keep adding in the same way until
you have the number you want.   Tie the threads
together (Fig.4). Leave thread "b" hanging down
(but remove the needle before you sit on it !)-
you will use it later on to add bead dangles,
loops or whatever else you want for the bottom
decoration.   Run thread "a" UP THRU THE SAME
bugle. You are ready to start the top triangle.

Put one bead on thread "a" and run thread thru
the loop between the last two bugles (Fig.5.).
Run the thread UP THRU THAT SAME bead (Fig.6.)
and pull it snug.

(Bugles separated)
(for better view.)

NOTE: Be careful in this
changing from Fig.5 to
Fig.6. This is the key
to this type of Peyote
stitch. The difference
is that the hole in the
bead points up from, not
across, the line of work.

Add another bead and go down thru
the next top loop (Fig.7.)then UP
and thru the bead (Fig.8.). Keep
repeating this to the end. There
will be one less beads in this row
than there are bugles in the base.

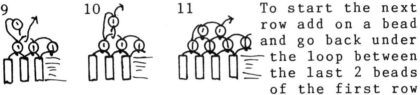

To start the next
row add on a bead
and go back under
the loop between
the last 2 beads
of the first row
(Fig. 9.). Pull it snug and go back UP thru it
(Fig.10.). Add the next bead (Fig.11.) in the
same way as you did for the
first row. Each new row
will have one less beads
than the one before it.
Keep adding rows until
you get down to two
beads as in (Fig.12.).

Here you need a loop for the ear wire.
To make it, add a loop of four or six (Fig.13).
For added strength, run a second thread thru the
loop as shown. To end the thread run down thru
several beads of the main piece and tie it down.
A small neat knot here and the top part is done.

Now put the needle back on thread
"b" and let's look at the bottom.
There you have a row of loops to
hang things from (Fig.14.). A
dangle is the easiest to make so
I have shown you how to make one (Fig.15.)

THAT is how I would teach you to make a
Bead Triangle if you were sitting here beside me.
You can see that this technique is a combination
of my ladder stitch and what I call the "Paiute"
altho others give it different names. After you
have mastered the thread pattern try making them
fancier with colored designs in the triangle and
combinations of loops and dangles for the bottom.

BEAD EMBROIDERY

1.　　　　In my classes I divide the teaching of Indian beadwork into three types.　　The first two, "Free-hand" chain-weaving and "Looming" I have already covered.　　The third which I call "Embroidery" is flatwork called by others under various names as Rosettes, Medallions, Applique, Sewn or Overlay.

2.　　　　Again, as in the other sections, I will concern myself with craft rather than art.　That is, I (as craftsman, not artist) plan to teach the techniques but the final designs are chosen, or developed, by the individual student.

46.　ROSETTES

3.　　　　The first difference we see is between circle-based work and pieces of mixed straight and curved lines. To start with the circular, I point out that one with eight separate sections (like pieces of pie)　is the easiest to make because that fits the shape of most seed beads. The first circle around the center has 8 beads, the second has 16 and each of the others has 8 more than the one before it (Fig. A).　Any variation　will be caused by bead size or tension irregularity.　The designs in the sections don't have to be the same but the bead arrangement will be.

4.　　　　It will be easier to build a design if you make a colored sketch of it first. That will prevent mistakes in arranging the colors as you pick up the beads.　　If the design is to be the same in all eight sections, a sketch of only one section is needed.

5.   Now to the work.   Some more experienced
beaders hold the base material
loosely,   but I find it easier
to work on if stretched firmly.
For rosette work I use a ply-
wood frame   (Fig. B)   with
material - leather, canvas, or
heavy cloth fastened with size
#1 ordinary carpet tacks.

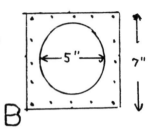

An embroidery hoop could substitute for a frame,
but if it snaps open you might
have trouble repositioning the
material with the same tension.

Draw four light pencil lines
meeting at the center (Fig.C).

6.   The center bead must be exactly at the
line intersection point and must be firmly tied.
(Fig. D).   Now bring the needle up
thru the material on
line "a" at a point
a half-bead distance from the
center bead. Pick up 8 beads.
Go on thru the first bead of
the eight and back down thru
a point on line "b" (Fig. E).
Draw it down tight and you have
the first circle (Fig.6) placed.   Fasten it down
firmly by sewing loops up
(Fig. F) and around the
thread at 2 or 3 places.
The first circle is done. (Fig.G).

7.   Do the same for the second circle.   Come
up again ON A LINE, pick up sixteen beads, go on
thru the first bead, as you did before, and down
thru the material. Now tack it firmly with loops
going up, around the thread, and back down. For
tight work I recommend a loop after every second
bead.   With this design base we will continue
with the outer circles.

8.   Now let's look at the commonest overlay
stitch, the"4-bead",
(Fig. H) thread up,
pick up four beads,
thread down, thread
goes back, then up between the second and
third beads, forward thru the third and fourth,
pick up four more and continue --- "down, back
two, forward thru two old beads, pick up four
new beads, repeat". Usually each section will
increase by one bead for each new circle added.
Don't be alarmed if you sometimes have to add
(or subtract) one bead because they are too
thick or thin.   Always keep your work snug.
(For several who asked how tight is "snug" ?
              snug = cuddle but don't squeeze !)

9.   The third and later circles use this
4-bead stitch. Since the UPs and DOWNs do not
all fall on section lines, you must be careful
in selection of beads (thick, normal, thin) so
that they will fit evenly into those lines.
Otherwise your finished piece will look ragged.
Start each circle even with a line.   When you
close a circle go on thru the first one or two
beads of that circle before going down so as
to have a smooth contact. Tie the thread with
a good knot (I use the one on Page 57) before
starting the next circle.

10.   The last circle
needs   special
work.   You can
use   either the
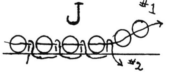
"2-bead" (Fig. I) or the "2-thread" (Fig. J)
stitch for it, and then finish by running the
thread around again thru the whole circle to get
all the beads in line.   If there are some beads
in the work that stick up from the others it is
because they have been crowded together too
tightly. Usually this can be corrected by extra
loops sewn around the thread next to the high
beads.

11.   If you have put the rosette on a bag or vest it is now done. If to be worn as a pendant it should have a leather backing. Glue a piece of "buck-skin" or other soft leather against the back of your work. If it is fairly large you may want to add some stiffness with a thin circle of plastic between the two materials.   If you do that,   leave a quarter-inch clearance around the edges for stitching.

12.   Be SURE that you have good glue contact, especially at edges.   Commercial glue made for "leather and cloth" should work.   After it has set well (over-night), rough-cut the leather and the base material a half-inch away from the bead- ing.   Then give it a fine-cut just even with the edge of the outer beads. Be very careful here so that you don't cut any threads.   You can now spiral stitch the two edges, leather & material, together or better yet, fasten them with a fancy beaded edging. Many variations of them are seen.

13.   Start any edging with one bead firmly set. Be very careful so that all stitches go thru both layers of material. The one-up edge (Fig. K) is the one most used. Sew the first bead, go back up and thru it.   Then the pattern is "pick-up two, down thru material, up and go back thru last bead, repeat". For something fancier, make up your own.   Some I have used are shown (Fig. L).   Any of these edging patterns can be added to edges of looming for belts,hatbands, headbands or bracelets).

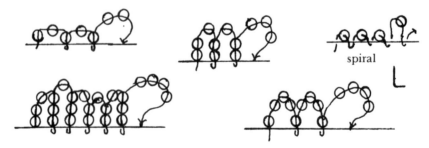

spiral

L

14.   Now your question must be, "Do I have to use eight sections ?".   Of course not. You don't

even have to use sections at all. But if you use
more or less than eight you can expect a problem
in fitting the beads to the lines. This can be
overcome by choosing thicker or thinner beads as
needed to make the result fit the guide lines.

47. FREE-SHAPED PIECES

15.   First make a pencil sketch (colored) of
the design that you want to make. Be careful
that the lines you draw are not too small to be
represented by the size of beads you are using.
Emphasize some of the major lines of the design
that can be used as guide-lines for filling in
the rest of the area.   Decide whether you are
going to work directly on a large piece of hand-
held material or, otherwise, on a smaller piece
which is stretched on a frame as shown in Fig.B.

16.   If you have gone thru the above section
on circles you already have most of the stitches
that you will need.   They
include the "4-bead"(Fig.H)
and the looser but similar
 "6-bead" (Fig. M) for
lines straight or nearly so. Then you have the
"2-bead" (Fig. I) or the "2-thread" (Fig. J)
for corners and tight curves. If you like the
"2-thread" you can also use it for 2 or 3 bead
units between the tie-loops in straight lines.
You will probably use the "4-bead" stitch more
than others for most of your embroidery pieces.

17.   Now you're ready to start beading.
 Start with a solid bead row along each of your
guide-lines. Then work on the supporting lines
beside them. When you come to a place where two
guide-lines meet at an angle fill the left-over
holes with single thinner beads placed sidewise
(as lines a & b, Fig. N).
When you have a series of
short (10 or less beads)
parallel lines (Fig. O)
to fill in, use a reverse
stitch.   (Fig. P).

18.   When the whole
piece is filled in, sew
down any "high" beads as
shown above.(para. 10)

       If you want several
parallel edge lines, put
them in next (warning :
sewing beads inside a curve is tricky -- it's
harder to get them firmly against it).   Finish
by extending the interior lines
to meet the outside edge beads.
If you have bubbles in the work
(single beads poking up) see
paragraph 10 for the solution.

19.   If your piece needs mounting (as for a
pendant) see paragraphs 11 and 12 for directions.
If to be appliqued on a bag or clothing, and the
sewing base is leather it can be fastened with a
spiral stitch after trimming the edges - glueing
is optional.   If the sewing base is canvas, I
recommend a thoro glueing to prevent edge-ravel.

48.   OTHER PATTERNS:

20.   SPOT STITCH:
                    Beading not filled in.
Outlines and enough interior lines to give the
desired image. Or partially beaded as flowers
and stems solidly beaded on an unbeaded background. Same sewing techniques as described in
paragraph 16.

21.   LAZY STITCH:
                  (Fig. Q)
It consists of wide rows each
composed of adjacent parallel
lines (usually 6 to 10 beads
long - Fig. R).   It is used
for solid cover of large areas. The loops at
ends of lines go down thru the base material

altho in high-grade Indian-made
pieces, the loops often go into
the base but not clear thru it.

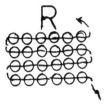

The lines lie loosely on the
base surface.

22. BEAD WRAPPING:

This is done around a
cylindrical base which is first prepared with
a wrapping of soft leather sewed on tightly.
The first circle of beads is put on with a
reversing stitch (as Fig. H or I) put in often
enough to keep the beads snug on the surface.
The fastest method then is to continue wrapping
spirelly with reverse stitches as needed.
Another method is to use the Peyote Tube
stitch shown on Page 27. To accomodate for the
base object becoming larger, you can put in two
real thin beads in one row in place of one bead
and put a new bead between them in the next row.
Do the opposite if the object is becoming smaller ; put two thin beads in normal places in one
row and then treat them as one in the next row.

23. EMBOSSING:

(Fig. S) This is an old-
time Indian technique very seldom, if ever, used
now. Some of them that I have
seen were obviously made for
"tourist" trade of long ago
(as boxes with beaded label
"BOX", whisk broom holder, picture frames, wall
container for matches). They are regarded as
antiques now. Their designs are usually related
to north-eastern tribes but an elderly Ojibwa
friend says her people used to make them. The
beads used are cut crystal, about size 5-7 ;
larger than "seed" beads. The lines are loose
and stand out definitely from the base surface.

(Reprint from the *MINNESOTA ARCHAEOLOGIST*, journal of the Minnesota Archaeology Society)

BEADS — An Essay

How to write briefly on a subject of real significance ? If by dimensions, then the most useful dimensions for describing Beads might be their History, their God-Thanking Use and their Techniques. Historically, glass beads have been used by Native Americans since they were first distributed along trade routes, by explorers, traders, clerics and rogues from Europe. Altho the various Tribes have had access to them for only 200 to 300 years, bead-working is regarded as a true Indian tradition because it has been developed from still earlier skills (shell, stone, wood and quill crafting) with little outside influence.

Our first thought as to meanings could be the Ojibwa name for seed beads - "Manido Minensug" - meaning "God's little berries". Also we can note that the English word "bead" comes directly from the Middle English "bede" meaning to pray. There is a pervading spiritual feeling in the use of beads - used much more to "say my heart" than to "look me pretty". Traditionally, Indians have used beads to add beauty and meaning to things for personal use (clothing, religious items, household articles).

For some Indians, bead-working represents a respect for their origin, their "Center", a tie with their peers and an attempt to convey to their children some concepts of a culture which is being eroded. For others, and for the "Wa-sheet-choo" (white man; outsider), beading is an interesting and instructive hobby thru which to gain some insight into the values of Native American cultures. And - it's FUN.

In building a piece of bead-work I use traditional designs, many of which have religious significance - and some of that has been shared with me by Indian friends. I develop

a spirit for the piece by thinking of the
pleasure I, or another, will get from having it

At the same time I know that others before
me have had a God-awareness while working with
symbols and that that God has taken many forms:
for Moses, for the Apostles, as well as the
Spirit who is approached by the Navajo Yei-Bichi,
the source of wisdom taught by the Crow symbolic
animals, the darting lights in a Lakota Sweat
Lodge, or the blessings bestowed by the Winnebago
Four Winds.

But aren't they all the same: "Grandfather"
of the sacred pipe ceremony taught by the White
Buffalo Calf Woman, "Jehovah" who appeared on
Sinai, and "Our Father" of Christian creeds ?

I want to include some words of Black Elk,
spiritual man of the Oglala, in explaining the
"Great Mystery": "You have noticed that everything an Indian does is in a circle. That is
because the Power of the World always works in
circles. The sky is round and I have heard that
the earth is round like a ball, and so are the
stars. The life of a man is a circle from childhood to childhood and so is everything where
power moves. Our tepees are round like the nests
of birds and these were always set in a circle.
The Nation is a nest of many nests where the
Great Spirit meant for us to hatch our children."

Now to Techniques: I first learned
beading by copying pieces that interested me. I
improved my work by studying my mistakes and thru
talking with Indian friends who were willing to
share a part of their culture with me. I learned
that different tribes can use different weaving
patterns to get the same design. This variety of
patterns has now intrigued me for many years and
has led to my retirement profession as a bead
teacher and to the distribution of my experience
in book form.

And now, "Grandfather - behold me and
the work of my hands -- help me to cast bright
shadows.
                Amen - Hola - so mote it be".

Bead-work by *Horace R. Goodhue*. Photography by *Jeanne Smith*.

Beaded Embroidery by *Horace R. Goodhue.* Photography by *Steve Skjold.*

Beaded Loom-work by *Horace R. Goodhue*. Photography by *Steve Skjold*.

Beaded Embroidery by *Horace R. Goodhue*. Photography by *Steve Skjold*.

ABOUT THE AUTHOR

HORACE R GOODHUE was born in western Minnesota, August 6, 1904. As a farm boy he acquired a love for nature and outdoor activities. He first learned about American Indian crafts as a member of the "Lone Scout" organization – a forerunner of the Boy Scouts. As a high school student in Northfield, Minnesota, he joined the Boy Scouts and eventually reached Eagle rank. Later as a Scoutmaster, he was invited into the Scouting fraternity, "Order of the Arrow" through which his interest in learning, preserving and teaching American Indian crafts was increased.

Mr. Goodhue's professional career began in 1926 as a graduate in Education and Mathematics from Carleton College in Northfield, Minnesota. He applied his degree as a teacher of Mathematics at Moorehead, Minnesota High School until 1942, when he joined the Army as an officer in his National Guard unit. During World War II he served overseas (ETO) as Commanding Officer (Lt. Col.), 22nd Anti-Aircraft Artillery Group. After being discharged, he enrolled in the University of Minnesota for a Graduate Degree in Counseling Psychology, which led to an appointment as a psychologist in the Veterans Administration Center at Fort Snelling, Minnesota. That location overlooks the Mdewakanton Dakota "Center of the World". Later, he was Chief of the Veterans Guidance Center for St. Paul Schools, and after that, Chief of the University of Minnesota Veterans Guidance Center. After leaving the Veterans Administration, Mr. Goodhue did family service work for the St. Paul International Institute, worked for the Minnesota Employment Service in veterans rehabilitation, and spent five years working in the St. Paul Post Office, from which he retired in 1966. Throughout these decades of work, his interest and passion for American Indian culture and bead-work grew.

Since retirement, over a period of a quarter of a century, Mr. Goodhue, accompanied by his wife Orpha, has spent several months each summer traveling throughout the country visiting American Indian communities and powwows to gain more knowledge of traditional bead-working. Through these experiences he has not only acquired an expertise which has led him to teach numerous classes and workshops on bead-working, but also respect and admiration from around the country as a recognized authority on beadcraft. His Ojibwa friends call him "Manidominensug Adewewinini" which translated literally means "he's the man who has God's little berries". Now, an octogenarian, Mr. Goodhue continues to teach and travel cross-country on a regular basis, further developing his knowledge of beading and sharing this knowledge with all who desire to learn some of the traditional American Indian ways.

Dear Beaders,

This reprinting is to honor my grandfather's love for beading and beaders everywhere. I want to to thank all of you for all the wonderful things written about my grandfather, Horace Goodhue.

His life was always a journey. There was always somewhere new to experience and new friends to meet. He loved life and got great pleasure in all the new adventures that beading took him. He loved all the great places he visited and the interesting people he met along the way. Who could have ever known the "hobby" he picked up in retirement could have led him to experience so many wonderful adventures and people. He and his wife, Orpha traveled during the summer in their motor home all across the country in search for the next great adventure. In the winter he would still have beading classes in the basement of their home. He attended many craft fairs and pow wows. He was also asked to be a speaker at many gatherings. He would aways be proud and in his full buckskin dance costume.

After his passing July 16, 1997 at 92, my grandmother Orpha's mission was to keep his legacy and love for beading alive. She did so until her passing in March of 2004. My mother, Janice was to be the next one to carry on his love for beading. Sadly, she passed the same day as Orpha, March 7, 2004.

I have been handed a great responsibility of carrying on all my grandfather did for his love for beading and beaders alive. I am able to do this along with the support and encouragement of my husband Eric and son Casey.

Thank you to all who knew and respected my grandfather and for continuing to learn the art of beading.

Happy Beading,

Jeanne Smith

INDEX

Zig-Zag Examples